"One cannot exaggerate the importance of the Eucharist for Christian, and especially Catholic, identity. All the more reason to praise Clifford Yeary's book, *Welcome to the Feast*. It hits just the right notes for a wide audience. Sophisticated yet not technical, it explores all the essential biblical foundations of the Eucharist. Yeary deftly interprets the pertinent Old and New Testament passages, summarizing the best scholarly interpretations in everyday language, while avoiding the trap of prooftexting. An informative *and* inspiring book I am pleased to recommend. It is a delectable little feast in itself!"

> Ronald D. Witherup, SS, superior general of the
> Sulpicians and author of *The Word of God at Vatican II:*
> *Exploring* Dei Verbum

"Great moments in biblical eating . . . this book traces the development of biblical eucharistic theology within the context of the deeper significance of meals in biblical narratives and ancient Mediterranean culture. Thoughtful reflections on the importance of food and eating in contemporary society complement readable and enriching commentary on this most important theme of Christian life."

> Carolyn Osiek, RSCJ
> Charles Fischer Professor of New Testament Emerita
> Brite Divinity School

"This book is indeed a feast. Cliff Yeary's prose flows so effortlessly that it is only upon reflection that the reader realizes the amazing amount of resources seamlessly woven together. This is a 'must have' for anyone teaching Eucharist and a refreshing update for all of us who celebrate Eucharist regularly."

> Irene Nowell is a Benedictine of Mount St. Scholastica
> in Atchison, Kansas

"*Welcome to the Feast* welcomes the reader into the richness of the biblical imagination. The interpretation of the stories of the Eucharist in Scripture fortifies with a fresh sense of understanding the chain of memory that Christians keep at the Table of the Lord. The conclusion of the book declares: 'May we always eat with hearts that give thanks.' What a fitting invitation offered by this inspiring book."

> Richard N. Fragomeni
> Professor of Liturgy and Preaching at The Catholic
> Theological Union, Chicago

Welcome to the Feast

The Story of the Eucharist in Scripture

Clifford Yeary

LITURGICAL PRESS
Collegeville, Minnesota

www.litpress.org

Nihil Obstat: Reverend Robert C. Harren, J.C.L., *Censor deputatus.*

Imprimatur: ✠ Most Reverend Donald J. Kettler, J.C.L.,
Bishop of St. Cloud, Minnesota. June 6, 2014.

Cover design by Ann Blattner. Image © Thinkstock by Getty Images.

Excerpts from the English translation of *The Roman Missal, Third Edition* © 2010, International Commission on English in the Liturgy Corporation (ICEL). All rights reserved.

1   2   3   4   5   6   7   8   9

Library of Congress Cataloging-in-Publication Data

Yeary, Clifford M.
    Welcome to the feast : the story of the eucharist in scripture / Clifford Yeary.
        pages   cm
    Includes bibliographical references.
    ISBN 978-0-8146-4969-5 — ISBN 978-0-8146-4994-7 (ebook)
        1. Lord's Supper—Biblical teaching.   2. Lord's Supper—Catholic Church.
    I. Title.

    BV825.3.Y43   2014
    234'.163—dc23

                                                          2014017727

In loving memory of
Fr. Robert Dabrowski, OFM Cap. (1910–1996),
a survivor of Dachau,

who welcomed me to my first feast at the Lord's table

on August 15, 1975.

Contents

Introduction   1

Chapter One
     Some Old Testament Feasts with God   3

Chapter Two
     A Wedding Feast in the Kingdom of God   19

Chapter Three
     The Last Supper   35

Chapter Four
     The Eucharist in Paul and Acts   54

Chapter Five
     The Eucharist and John's Gospel   71

Conclusion   86

Suggested Readings   88

Introduction

Among the more liturgically oriented Christian faith traditions, the Eucharist is central to faith and worship. As a Catholic, I am deeply appreciative of how Catholic teaching concerning the Eucharist continues to enrich my faith in untold ways. This commentary, however, was not undertaken in order to "prove" that Catholic doctrines on the Eucharist are to be explicitly found in the Bible. Rather, I hope to assist those without theological degrees to gain insight and appreciation for the deep biblical roots of the Eucharist. Those biblical roots are richly nourishing and those who know what their faith teaches will recognize the vital relationship between their traditions and the scriptural accounts.

I have been engaged in serious study of Scripture for many years and have always called myself a student of Scripture while disclaiming the title of scholar. In this commentary my goal is to open up the Scriptures to the best of my ability while providing you, the reader, with the rich gleanings from many respected scholars. In discussions specifically dealing with the Eucharist in the New Testament, I have relied solely on Catholic Scripture scholars. I am grateful to all for helping me engage with the biblical accounts about encounters with God and the Son of God during the very human experience of eating a meal. As this commentary is directed toward general readers, I have avoided the use of footnotes, but in fairness to the scholars with whose ideas I engage, I have tried to consistently inform you of the sources I used. At the back of the book you will find a list of the most pertinent names in a recommended reading list.

It may come as a surprise that in the opening chapter I begin with Abraham and Sarah and the hospitality they showed when three strangers who were imbued with a divine aura appeared at their tent. But that is how the story that builds up to the Eucharist in the New Testament begins, with the desire of both God and people to be in intimate fellowship with each other in the context of a meal. God gives us food for the nurturing of our lives, but the greatest nurture of all is God's presence at a meal. Later, in the Old Testament, we learn that the blessings God promises the children of Israel are an invitation to a feast, a wedding feast, in which their God will be united with them as a loving, devoted spouse. When Jesus began to minister to the people of Israel, he consistently invited them to feast with him as their bridegroom. His ministry culminated in a meal in which he offered bread and wine as his own body and blood soon to be taken and shed in a violent execution on a cross.

He asked that his followers continue to offer this meal "in memory of me," and this they remembered to do after he had risen from the dead, making that memory of him one of deep sorrow and yet of unsurpassable joy. And so we too are invited to eat with the Savior, to remember his passion and resurrection in the breaking of bread. Therefore let us faithfully respond to his call as we are bidden, *Welcome to the feast!*

CHAPTER ONE

Some Old Testament Feasts with God

The Hospitality of Abraham

Genesis 18:1-15

Abraham's Visitors. ¹The LORD appeared to Abraham by the oak of Mamre, as he sat in the entrance of his tent, while the day was growing hot. ²Looking up, he saw three men standing near him. When he saw them, he ran from the entrance of the tent to greet them; and bowing to the ground, ³he said: "Sir, if it please you, do not go on past your servant. ⁴Let some water be brought, that you may bathe your feet, and then rest under the tree. ⁵Now that you have come to your servant, let me bring you a little food, that you may refresh yourselves; and afterward you may go on your way." "Very well," they replied, "do as you have said."

⁶Abraham hurried into the tent to Sarah and said, "Quick, three measures of bran flour! Knead it and make bread." ⁷He ran to the herd, picked out a tender, choice calf, and gave it to a servant, who quickly prepared it. ⁸Then he got some curds and milk, as well as the calf that had been prepared, and set these before them, waiting on them under the tree while they ate.

⁹"Where is your wife Sarah?" they asked him. "There in the tent," he replied. ¹⁰One of them said, "I will return to you about this time next year, and Sarah will then have a son." Sarah was listening at the entrance of the tent, just behind him. ¹¹Now Abraham and Sarah were old, advanced in years, and Sarah had stopped having her menstrual

periods. [12]So Sarah laughed to herself and said, "Now that I am worn out and my husband is old, am I still to have sexual pleasure?" [13]But the LORD said to Abraham: "Why did Sarah laugh and say, 'Will I really bear a child, old as I am?' [14]Is anything too marvelous for the LORD to do? At the appointed time, about this time next year, I will return to you, and Sarah will have a son." [15]Sarah lied, saying, "I did not laugh," because she was afraid. But he said, "Yes, you did."

At the time the three strangers approach Abraham at the oak of Mamre, this aging couple have left their original homeland in order to faithfully respond to a call from God (Gen 12:1). God has promised that the entire region of Canaan would be the inheritance of Abraham's offspring through Sarah (at least by implication), and yet they have grown old and have had no children together. There is no hint, however, that their hospitality toward these strangers is provided in expectation of any sort of gift or repayment.

In the New Testament, Abraham and Sarah's hospitality to these three strangers is most probably responsible for the exhortation in the Letter to the Hebrews urging Christians to be hospitable people, for through hospitality "some have unknowingly entertained angels" (13:2).

While nothing is explicitly said about whether Abraham recognized the angelic or divine nature of his visitors, Abraham is someone who has been visited by God more than once (see Gen 12:7-9; 15:1-20; 17:1-22). We also have to consider that the appearance of God to Abraham by "the oak of Mamre" would not have happened coincidentally. In ancient times special trees of the region, some called oaks and others terebinths, were considered likely places for religious encounters and would be the place markers for a variety of religious activities, including sacrifices to other gods that drew the ire of prophets long after the time of Abraham (see Isa 1:29 and Hos 4:13).

Many of God's appearances in Genesis are said to be anthropomorphic, that is to say, they depict God as having a human form and in many ways displaying human behavior (see Gen 3:8) and so God's appearing to Abraham in human form here should not surprise us. What is most curious about this particular appearance to Abraham, though, is that while it is said that it is the Lord who appears to Abraham, we learn that it is three men that Abraham sees standing near him.

Some scholars explain this by suggesting that we have two traditions being blended into one account. One tradition has the Lord appearing to Abraham while another tradition tells of three men, all of whom would be thought of as angels of the LORD. Richard J. Clifford, in *The New Jerome Biblical Commentary*, suggests that the singularity of God and the plurality of figures work together to express both God's nearness and elusiveness. In other words, God's appearance to Abraham was very real, but it is impossible to adequately describe the event, and the somewhat confusing issue of how many figures Abraham entertained is all part of the spiritual aura surrounding the encounter.

Christians have always read the Old Testament in light of faith's assurance that Jesus Christ is the center of God's revelation. After all, we read in Luke that it was the risen Christ himself who taught the apostles to seek Christ in reading the Sacred Scriptures of the Jewish people: " 'These are my words that I spoke to you while I was still with you, that everything written about me in the law of Moses and in the prophets and psalms must be fulfilled.' Then he opened their minds to understand the scriptures" (24:44-45).

During the Council of Constantinople in AD 381, the Christian church declared that belief in the Holy Trinity was an essential aspect of authentic faith in Christ. Eventually, reading the Old Testament as Christian revelation, and explicit belief in the triune nature of God, led the early-fifteenth-century Russian mystic Andrei Rublev to portray the three "men" who visited Abraham by the oak of Mamre as an encounter with the Holy Trinity. It is arguably the most famous icon of all time.

Catholic and Protestant biblical scholars alike are far more careful today to attempt to read and interpret the Old Testament texts within historical and literary contexts from which they arose. At the time the narrative of the encounter between Abraham and the three figures was put into its present form, there was no awareness of or belief in a trinity of persons in God. This modern, scholarly approach also allows for a faithful reading of the Old Testament that leads us to Christ, however. It does so as it traces the growth and development of a burning desire among Abraham's offspring for a redeeming presence of God that would call all peoples into relationship with Israel's God (see Tob 13:11; Ps 87; Isa 42:6-7; Jer 3:14-17; Mic 4:2-3; Zech 2:14-15). This aspiration for communion with God in the Old Testament is one that early Jewish followers of Jesus believed God had granted them in Jesus, their Messiah, and that has remained the belief of Christians throughout time.

So, while it is wise to be aware of the historical and literary contexts of biblical accounts when interpreting their theological thrust, it would also be foolish to ignore how biblical texts of earlier eras helped form and fashion later believers' understanding of their faith.

We can safely assert, therefore, that Rublev's icon of the Old Testament Trinity rightly continues to invite Christians into a deep contemplation of the mystery of God's self-revelation to Abraham and Sarah. In their depictions of the meeting between God and Abraham at the oak of Mamre, both the Genesis account and Rublev's icon open us to the journey of faith that leads Christians to eventually discover the triune nature of God and more: they also point us in the direction of the Eucharist. In Abraham and Sarah's gracious hospitality toward the divine visitors there is an early stirring of the pervasive biblical appetite for communion with this God who would dine at table with us in mutual hospitality.

Notice how the title "LORD" is printed in this verse (Gen 18:1): "The LORD appeared to Abraham by the oak of Mamre." Whenever we see the word "LORD" printed out in capital letters in the Old Testament, it is the translators' customary way of alerting us to the presence in the Hebrew text of the special name of God, *Yahweh*, a name that another tradition held was not made known until it was revealed to Moses from the burning bush (Exod 3:1-15). Because the name of God is to be held in the highest respect and in due deference to the commandment not to take the name of God in vain (Exod 20:7), most English translations of the Old Testament have honored the ancient Jewish tradition of reading "LORD" (*Adonai* in Hebrew) instead of "Yahweh" when the latter appears in the Hebrew text.

Along with questions about when the name "Yahweh" was revealed (does its presence in the Abraham narratives contradict the narrative of its revelation to Moses in the burning bush? [see Gen 12:8]), the meaning of this name has also been a subject of great interest. While it is often translated into English as "I AM" or cryptically as "I am who I am" (Exod 3:14), the enduring inference surrounding this name is what God tells Moses in Exodus 3:12: "I will be with you." Regardless of when the name was revealed, the God who appears to Abraham at the oak of Mamre is deliberately identified with the God who is revealed to Moses at the burning bush. This is a God who makes promises and keeps them, by being with us throughout our journeys through life. The God who was revealed to Abraham and Moses is a God who will always be with his people.

For Christians, this revelation reaches its climax in the person of Jesus Christ, who is revealed to us as "Emmanuel," which literally means "God with us" (see Matt 1:23).

In this account of Abraham and Sarah's hospitality toward the three strangers we discover that true hospitality comes from God, who seeks to be with us and binds himself to us in a covenant filled with promise. In this account, the promise is that Sarah will bear a son in a year's time, a son who will be the essential link between Abraham and Sarah and the generations to come who will form the body of God's covenant people.

What is it about food that a meal can both be the instrument of a vital communion with God and provide the occasion for receiving the most important of God's promises to us?

Today, many are unaware of the great theological and anthropological significance of food in our lives. Perhaps that is because it is so easy to take food for granted in our consumer culture. In fact, for many, food has become a threat to well-being, as the abundance of food within our reach can place us at risk for obesity, diabetes, and heart disease. That is not to say we don't love food—just the opposite—but we are in danger, as a culture, of forgetting some of the most important values that should surround our eating and drinking.

Eating and drinking, at the most basic level, are what keep us alive. Only breathing is more important to us, and if we don't eat and drink enough, we will, in a matter of a few weeks or less, quit breathing. Hunger and malnutrition are serious problems not only in impoverished areas of the world, but a surprising percentage of Americans, many of them children, face daily challenges in obtaining their nutritional needs. Ironically, it is the poor who are most likely to suffer from both obesity and malnutrition in America: the cheaper the food, the less nutritious it is.

While we eat to stay alive, it is eating for pleasure that powers the business engine behind our food. Marketing mavens know how to tickle our taste buds, tempting us to eat any time of day. We eat in our cars, at our desks, while watching television, when we are excited and when we are bored. We may even eat to compensate for other unfulfilled needs in our life.

Today, many of us eat alone even when eating in public. Eating in a fast-food restaurant can place us side by side any number of strangers without it becoming a social event.

Today, many families can go days without sitting down at a table and sharing a common meal. Our schedules are crammed with important activities and eating simply becomes a necessity. A pleasurable necessity, but one that can be accommodated with such ease that it needn't engage us socially with anyone, even our families. Now, with the advent of smartphones and other mini-sized computers, it is not uncommon to deliberately or unconsciously avoid personal contact with family members on those occasions when we do eat at the same table with each other.

There are still those special occasions when eating does become a celebration of life shared with others. Thanksgiving and the holy days of Christmas and Easter still have that importance for many. A meal celebrating a wedding anniversary might not only renew the bond between a couple, but silver and golden anniversaries are often feasts for extended families and friends across many generations. There are also special occasions without fixed annual dates, such as weddings and funerals, baptisms and confirmations, all key moments in life and death for which meals are shared.

These special occasions, when food is both the sign and nurturer of our social and familial bonds with loved ones, are vital to this study of Eucharist in Scripture. When we bring our own experiences of being drawn into deeper communion with others in our lives through food, we have "tasted" an appetizer for that ultimate meal of communion between God and ourselves.

As a culture, it may seem that we have come a long way from the day of Abraham and Sarah, when the hospitality of offering food to strangers on a journey meant the sharing of life itself, and brought with it the divine promise of new life. There are many among us who continue this practice of hospitality to strangers, however. They serve strangers in soup kitchens, feed families through food banks, and deliver nutrition to the starving around the world through charitable organizations.

Abraham and Sarah are unique, though, in that their hospitality welcomed God into the world in a way that initiates the story of our salvation. In the context of the book of Genesis, until Abraham and Sarah's faithful reception of God into their lives, the Almighty had seemed almost powerless to repair the damage humans had wrought in their relationship with the Creator. The narratives that precede the accounts of Abraham and Sarah—those of Adam and Eve (Gen 3), Cain and Abel (Gen 4:1-16), and the tower of Babel (Gen 11:1-9)—all tell the story of humanity's failures. In the account of Noah and the Flood we learn that God utterly gave up on humankind except for Noah and his family, but the flood no sooner dries up than Noah and his family launch the return of evil into the world (Gen 6:5–9:27).

Up until Abraham, God seems to deal with humanity as a whole and little good seems to come of it. With Abraham and Sarah, however, God becomes far more personal and the attempts to repair humanity's relationship with God begin in earnest. Although humans now cover the face of the earth, it is just this one man and one woman through whom God will now begin to unveil the plan to restore all humanity into harmony with himself.

That Abraham recognizes the divine nature of his visitors is hinted at in the contrast between his invitation to dine with him and the course that he has prepared for them. "[L]et me bring you *a little food*" (emphasis mine), he tells them, but then we read, "Abraham hurried into the tent to Sarah and said, 'Quick, three measures of bran flour! Knead it and make bread.' He ran to the herd, picked out a tender, choice calf, and gave it to a servant, who quickly prepared it. Then he got some curds and milk, as well as the calf that had been prepared, and set these before them, waiting on them under the tree while they ate" (Gen 18:5-8).

Apparently it is Abraham, and not his servant, who waits on the trio who dine under the tree.

For Christians, the entire sweep of salvation history seems symbolically captured in one brief detail found in 18:4. Abraham's hospitality includes having his guests' feet washed, the cultural refreshment provided to weary journeyers of the region throughout history. We will note this custom again when we ponder the Eucharist in the Gospel of John. Suffice it to note now that Abraham directs that water be brought to them so that their feet can be washed. As hospitable as he is, the washing of their feet is not something that Abraham will personally undertake. It will take a far humbler person than Abraham to undertake this demeaning role (see John 13:1-17).

Modern readers bring modern sensibilities to ancient texts such as this one, and so are likely to notice that while Abraham is very hospitable and does indeed humble himself to serve his guests, his wife, all the while, is confined to the tent. In the culture of the time (which has not changed that much in many parts of the world), Sarah, for all her labors in preparing the food for these guests, would probably be thought of as merely extending Abraham's hospitality. But her importance to the narrative is nevertheless critical. Without Sarah, the promise to Abraham found in Genesis 12:3 that "All the families of the earth will find blessing in you" will not be fulfilled. Abraham already has a son, Ishmael, but only a son through Sarah will fulfill God's promise (Gen 17:18-19). And so, it is in the course of this meal, which Sarah has helped prepare, that the imminent fulfillment of this promise is announced.

Nothing tells us that the three visitors, in their altogether human guise, are recognized by Abraham as familiar guests. They are strangers, but strangers in whom Abraham senses the presence of the divine and who, therefore, receive the finest hospitality he can provide. These guests—or one of them at least—know(s) Abraham very well, however (we read plainly of the close-knit relationship of the divine visitor to Abraham in Genesis 18:16-33), and so the reader is not taken by surprise when one of them asks Abraham where his wife, Sarah, is. Since Sarah's "place," especially during a visit of male strangers, is in the tent, asking about her whereabouts is partly rhetorical, but that the stranger knows the name of his wife is a sign of his divine nature. Nothing in the narrative tells us that Abraham has named his wife to his visitors.

While Sarah, for her part, does not break out of the prevailing culture's sensibilities by leaving the tent, that does not mean she intends to remain aloof from this visitation. She keeps an ear, it would seem, to the flap of the tent in close proximity to the visitors, so that she will miss nothing of what is going on. And so she hears the promise as it is announced. When the key stranger returns to visit in a year's time, the male heir promised to Abraham through his wife Sarah will have arrived. It is this announcement by a certain "one" of the visitors that removes all doubt that Abraham is being visited by Yahweh.

When Sarah hears it, she laughs and her laughter is overheard. Sarah is not just disbelieving in this all-important moment when the divine nature of the visitor has been revealed. Her laughter scoffs at God's promise. The Lord asks why Sarah has laughed, and knowing that she has been heard, she denies it, which seems a very foolish thing to do, given who has overheard it. But Sarah has her own human predicament to anchor her disbelief: she has gone through menopause and no longer expects to have sexual relations with her husband.

To be sure, Sarah is not alone in her laughter. In Genesis 17:15-17, when God promises Abraham that he will have an heir and that Sarah is the one who will bear him, it is Abraham who laughs because of the ridiculousness of his and Sarah's ages. While we may understand the Lord's response to Sarah's laughter as a rebuke ("Is anything too marvelous for the LORD to do?" [18:14]), it is also a reassurance that the birth of the heir will come about. The laughter of both Abraham and Sarah is also far more than disbelief in the promise. Their laughter is a harbinger of the joy they will have in the birth of their son, Isaac, whose name means "laughter."

This hospitable banquet shared between Abraham and the three visitors is foundational for the entire sweep of salvation history found in both the Old Testament and New. It is through Abraham and Sarah's offspring that the one who will fulfill all God's promises will eventually be born. In anticipating the prophetic role of John the Baptist—another child conceived through divine promise to elderly parents—Zechariah prays in remembrance of Abraham's all important role:

Luke 1:68-75

> [68]"Blessed be the Lord, the God of Israel,
>   for he has visited and brought redemption to his people.
> [69]He has raised up a horn for our salvation
>   within the house of David his servant,
> [70]even as he promised through the mouth of his holy prophets from of old:
>   [71]salvation from our enemies and from the hand of all who hate us,
> [72]to show mercy to our fathers
>   and to be mindful of his holy covenant
> [73]and of the oath he swore to Abraham our father,
>   and to grant us that,
> [74]rescued from the hand of enemies,
>   without fear we might worship him
> [75]in holiness and righteousness
>   before him all our days.

The Passover

Exodus 12:1-30

The Passover Ritual Prescribed. [1]The LORD said to Moses and Aaron in the land of Egypt: [2]This month will stand at the head of your calendar; you will reckon it the first month of the year. [3]Tell the whole community of Israel: On the tenth of this month every family must procure for itself a lamb, one apiece for each household. [4]If a household is too small for a lamb, it along with its nearest neighbor will procure one, and apportion the lamb's cost in proportion to the number of persons, according to what each household consumes. [5]Your lamb must be a year-old male and without blemish. You may take it from either the sheep or the goats. [6]You will keep it until the fourteenth day of this month, and then, with the whole community of Israel assembled, it will be slaughtered during the evening twilight. [7]They will take some of its blood and apply it to the two doorposts and the lintel of the houses in which they eat it. [8]They will consume its meat that same night, eating it roasted with unleavened bread and bitter herbs. [9]Do not eat any of it raw or even boiled in water, but roasted, with its head and shanks and inner organs. [10]You must not keep any of it beyond the morning; whatever is left over in the morning must be burned up.

[11]This is how you are to eat it: with your loins girt, sandals on your feet and your staff in hand, you will eat it in a hurry. It is the LORD's Passover. [12]For on this same night I will go through Egypt, striking down every firstborn in the land, human being and beast alike, and executing judgment on all the gods of Egypt—I, the LORD! [13]But for you the blood will mark the houses where you are. Seeing the blood, I will pass over you; thereby, when I strike the land of Egypt, no destructive blow will come upon you.

[14]This day will be a day of remembrance for you, which your future generations will celebrate with pilgrimage to the LORD; you will celebrate it as a statute forever. [15]For seven days you must eat unleavened bread. From the very first day you will have your houses clear of all leaven. For whoever eats leavened bread from the first day to the seventh will be cut off from Israel. [16]On the first day you will hold a sacred assembly, and likewise on the seventh. On these days no sort of work shall be done, except to prepare the food that everyone needs. [17]Keep, then, the custom of the unleavened bread, since it was on this very day that I brought your armies out of the land of Egypt. You must observe this day throughout your generations as a statute forever. [18]From the evening of the fourteenth day of the first month until the evening of the twenty-first day of this month you will eat unleavened bread. [19]For seven days no leaven may be found in your houses; for anyone, a resident alien or a native, who eats leavened food will be cut off from the community of Israel. [20]You shall eat nothing leavened; wherever you dwell you may eat only unleavened bread.

Promulgation of the Passover. [21]Moses summoned all the elders of Israel and said to them, "Go and procure lambs for your families, and slaughter the Passover victims. [22]Then take a bunch of hyssop, and dipping it in the blood that is in the basin, apply some of this blood to the lintel and the two doorposts. And none of you shall go outdoors until morning. [23]For when the LORD goes by to strike down the Egyptians, seeing the blood on the lintel and the two doorposts, the LORD will pass over that door and not let the destroyer come into your houses to strike you down.

[24]"You will keep this practice forever as a statute for yourselves and your descendants. [25]Thus, when you have entered the land which the LORD will give you as he promised, you must observe this rite. [26]When your children ask you, 'What does this rite of yours mean?' [27]you will reply, 'It is the Passover sacrifice for the LORD, who passed over the houses of the Israelites in Egypt; when he struck down the Egyptians, he delivered our houses.'"

Then the people knelt and bowed down, [28]and the Israelites went and did exactly as the LORD had commanded Moses and Aaron.

Death of the Firstborn. ²⁹And so at midnight the LORD struck down every firstborn in the land of Egypt, from the firstborn of Pharaoh sitting on his throne to the firstborn of the prisoner in the dungeon, as well as all the firstborn of the animals. ³⁰Pharaoh arose in the night, he and all his servants and all the Egyptians; and there was loud wailing throughout Egypt, for there was not a house without its dead.

From within the context of the biblical narrative, the Passover marks the onset of the fulfillment of an early promise of God made to Abram before changing his name to Abraham: "Then the LORD said to Abram: Know for certain that your descendants will reside as aliens in a land not their own, where they shall be enslaved and oppressed for four hundred years. But I will bring judgment on the nation they must serve, and after this they will go out with great wealth" (Gen 15:13-14).

The events of the Passover are those that led to the liberation of the Hebrew slaves from Egypt. Passover marks the beginning of their deliverance from oppression and the flight from Egypt that would take them to a land of both freedom and prosperity. Because of the Passover, they are now free to be a people uniquely dedicated to the God who liberates them (see Exod 12:1-17).

There are a number of rituals associated with a Passover meal, including questions posed by children concerning the reasons for using each specific item of the set menu. Through these rituals, prayers, and blessings, and in the eating of the meal itself, the participants come to a vital understanding of the importance of the Passover to their lives. From a Jewish perspective, those who eat the Passover meal to this day are not only celebrating the historical significance for the children of Abraham at the first Passover, but they are, in fact, participating in the saving events of Passover itself. They actually encounter the Passover event and become living witnesses to its liberating effects. Eating the Passover is itself an act of liberation. The freedom to worship God as part of a people specifically called into a covenant relationship with God is at the very heart of what it means to be a Jew in Jesus' day as well as today.

Exodus 12:1-20 actually describes two religious feasts, the Passover and the feast of Unleavened Bread. The Passover meal is eaten on the evening of a single particular day, while the eating of unleavened bread continues for an entire week. Scholars of the Old Testament tell us that both the Passover meal and the feast of Unleavened Bread may well have predated their association with the exodus. The ritual slaughtering of a male lamb is thought to have been associated with the annual moving of the flock in the spring. The feast of Unleavened Bread is mentioned twice in association with the exodus (23:15 and 34:18) without mention of the Passover. It is believed that the feast of Unleavened Bread began as a harvest celebration.

This in no way suggests that their biblical association with the exodus is to be faulted. The exodus is the foundational experience in the memory of Israel from which they date their liberation from oppression and slavery in Egypt and their clear emergence as the covenanted people of God. That two festivals predating the exodus became the particular feasts dedicated to celebrating God's deliverance tells us that those earlier feasts forever lost their earlier significance in light of the intimate association they gained with the exodus.

We would not call this feast of lamb, bitter herbs, and unleavened bread "fast food," but everything about it is associated with the exodus in a way to remind all succeeding generations that their ancestors fled in haste from the land of their enslavement. They are to eat with their robes hitched up for running, their staff in hand for support over rough terrain, and the unleavened nature of the bread (matzoth) reminds again that they had no time to wait for their bread to rise before baking it. Even the bitter herbs are there to remind them of the bitterness of their former oppression.

There are definite overtones of sacrifice in the slaying of a lamb for the Passover. It is the blood of lamb on the doorposts of the Hebrew households that causes the "destroyer" to bypass them (Exod 12:21-24). And in Deuteronomy 16:1-5 it is actually called a sacrifice and the killing of the lambs are to eventually take place in the temple, that is, "in the place the LORD will choose as the dwelling place of his name."

It is generally accepted by Old Testament scholars that Deuteronomy was compiled as late as the reign of King Josiah, some six centuries after the exodus. This tells us that the Passover grew in cultic significance over time. The repurposing and adaptation of the Passover in the life of God's people is nowhere so vividly evident, though, as in the Synoptic Gospels (Matthew, Mark, and Luke), when Jesus' celebration of the Passover with his disciples before his death becomes his Last Supper. The Jewish feast of Passover becomes, in the life of the church, the celebration of Eucharist.

This is a transformation so great that the Jewish Passover Jesus celebrates at the Last Supper in Matthew, Mark, and Luke only peripherally recalls the exodus from Egypt. In their gospels, this Passover meal is now indelibly stamped with the passion and resurrection of Jesus as its primary reference. As Luke recounts Moses' and Elijah's discussion with

Jesus at the transfiguration, the ultimate "exodus" is the one Jesus undertakes for us on the cross (see Luke 9:29-31). It must be stressed, however, that Jesus' exodus does not diminish the greatness of the original. It is the great spiritual importance of Israel's exodus that brings Moses and Elijah (in Luke) to call Jesus' death and resurrection an exodus.

The Gospel of John will directly associate Jesus' death with the Passover by his references to Jesus as "the Lamb of God" (1:29, 36), and by stating that Jesus died on the day of preparation for the Passover, the very hour the Passover lambs were being slaughtered in the temple. We will discuss the discrepancy between John and the Synoptic Gospels concerning the timing of the Passover and the Last Supper in a later chapter.

For now, let us recall that the Passover itself is a meal of great promise, a meal that launched the people of God into a new life of freedom and covenant relationship with God. This is a meal that the Jewish people have eaten throughout the ages in the hope that they will always remain free to worship God while enjoying all the gifts and promises God gave them in the exodus. And then, let us ponder the tragic fact that they often found themselves less than free. The Passover meal can be a reminder to Christians that freedom of religion is a right belonging to all people for all time, as the Vatican II document *Dignitatis Humanae* teaches.

A Feast for the Ages

Isaiah 25:6-10b

The exodus is often dated around 1200 BC. The prophet scholars refer to as First Isaiah lived nearly five hundred years later, long after the Israelites had settled into the Promised Land, three hundred years or so after the glorious biblical depictions of the reigns of Kings David and Solomon. In Isaiah's time, around 740–700 BC, Jerusalem and its environs came under attack and were nearly destroyed.

Sometimes things look so bad there's no way to imagine anything other than the pain and suffering that is being experienced. Walter Brueggemann, one of the most respected Old Testament scholars of our time, tells us that chapters 24–27 of Isaiah were probably written during just such a time in Jerusalem's history. Unfortunately, there were many specific tragic events that befell Jerusalem and Judah during this time. Identifying the precise circumstances during which these prophecies are set is impossible. One likely possibility, however, could have been an Assyrian invasion of Judah in 701 BC, just before the end of Isaiah's career. The Assyrian leader Sennacherib claimed to have destroyed forty-six cities in Judah as well as countless villages before laying siege to Jerusalem. People would starve to death during sieges and one is welcome to wonder if it was during just such conditions that Isaiah pronounced the outlandish promises of 25:6-10b.

> ⁶On this mountain the LORD of hosts
>   will provide for all peoples
> A feast of rich food and choice wines,
>   juicy, rich food and pure, choice wines.
> ⁷On this mountain he will destroy
>   the veil that veils all peoples,
> The web that is woven over all nations.
>   ⁸He will destroy death forever.
> The Lord God will wipe away
>   the tears from all faces;
> The reproach of his people he will remove
>   from the whole earth; for the LORD has spoken.
>   ⁹On that day it will be said:
> "Indeed, this is our God; we looked to him, and he saved us!
>   This is the LORD to whom we looked;
>   let us rejoice and be glad that he has saved us!" . . .
> ¹⁰For the hand of the LORD will rest on this mountain . . .

What was a luxuriant joy that people couldn't imagine in their distress, the prophet saw as God's ultimate intention for them. This is the same prophet that warned them repeatedly that unimaginable woes were about to befall them because they had let the poor starve and denied justice to widows and orphans and rejected Yahweh for foreign idols. Then, suddenly, in the midst of the promised grievous plight, the prophet announces a future of incredible bliss: "A feast of rich food and choice wines." It extends God's promises of a bounteous feast to "all peoples."

This is no small vision. Along with the feasting on rich food and choice wines, there is an end to death. The revised New American Bible translation states that God will also destroy "the veil that veils all peoples." This veil is, according to Brueggemann, a death shroud, and the shroud of death is not simply destroyed; it is "swallowed" in Hebrew. The theme of feasting for all peoples is echoed in God's act of swallowing death. The death that is swallowed up by God is not just physical death. This death is a web woven over all peoples, ensnaring the living and impeding life from being lived to the fullest. The promised feast will bring fullness of life and will bring it to everyone, Jew and Gentile alike. In

Isaiah's time, when Gentile nations were threatening the very existence of Judah, such a promise would have been mind-boggling.

The promise is, in fact, apocalyptic. The future it envisions cannot be reconciled with the historical realities of the time, which is what makes it an apocalyptic vision. Apocalypses are not always things of gloom and doom. In the Bible, apocalypses usually end in salvation and healing with a world finally set right with God, never to fear judgment again. Such is this apocalyptic vision. It is a vision not just for Israel, but for all the peoples of the world.

This prophecy creates an apocalyptic hope in anyone who trusts it as the word of God. It nurtured hope in a tormented people for a time when God's will for life, peace, and justice would hold absolute sway on earth. This is a time that would be known as the kingdom of God. At the heart of that vision would always be the image of a feast. Certainly, in Jesus' time, there were those who hoped for the onset of the kingdom of God and that when it arrived they would be invited to the feast celebrating it. Later, we will discuss how the many meals Jesus ate with sinners were also closely associated with the kingdom of God.

A century after the Isaiah who lived during Sennacherib's invasion, another prophet in the tradition of Isaiah (Second Isaiah) renewed the vision of a feast in the kingdom of God at a time when Jerusalem lay in ruins and the people of Judah were exiles in Babylon.

Rich Fare at No Cost

Isaiah 55:1-5

> [1]All you who are thirsty,
>> come to the water!
> You who have no money,
>> come, buy grain and eat;
> Come, buy grain without money,
>> wine and milk without cost!
> [2]Why spend your money for what is not bread;
>> your wages for what does not satisfy?
> Only listen to me, and you shall eat well,
>> you shall delight in rich fare.
> [3]Pay attention and come to me;
>> listen, that you may have life.
> I will make with you an everlasting covenant,
>> the steadfast loyalty promised to David.
> [4]As I made him a witness to peoples,
>> a leader and commander of peoples,

> [5]So shall you summon a nation you knew not,
>   and a nation that knew you not shall run to you,
> Because of the LORD, your God,
>   the Holy One of Israel, who has glorified you.

Once again a future feast is proclaimed, one, however, that is hinged upon dutiful attention to the divine host: "Only listen to me . . . Pay attention and come to me; / listen, that you may have life." Through the prophet, God is calling all the exiles to return to Jerusalem and he will feed them with a rich banquet. Their coming to Jerusalem is part of their obligation to come to God. Along with the feast, they are promised an everlasting covenant and the assurance that, instead of their present subjection to foreign powers, they will be the ones to summon other nations.

There is a metaphorical aspect to this banquet, for it is God who is to be drink to their souls. In John's gospel, it will be at the end of a major feast, the feast of Tabernacles, that Jesus will practically quote Isaiah 55:1: "Let anyone who thirsts come to me and drink" (John 7:37).

The banquet promised in Isaiah 55 is also closely linked to the promise of that time to be known as the kingdom of God. If the people listen to God and come to him (and to Jerusalem), they will be offered an everlasting covenant. In Second Samuel, God made an everlasting covenant with David: "Your house and your kingdom are firm forever before me; your throne shall be firmly established forever" (2 Sam 7:16). At the time of the promise of an everlasting covenant here in Isaiah, there is no kingdom of Israel, let alone a throne of David. But the people have not forgotten the promise made to David and neither has the Lord. So it is that God is renewing the people's expectation of a kingdom in which God's rule will be forever established. This entails not just a renewal of God's covenant with David, for this is an additional covenant like the everlasting one God made with David. This everlasting covenant, however, God will make with the people, not just with their king. Such a covenant, such a kingdom, will be forever etched in the minds of God's people in association with a feast of royal proportions. It is a banquet to which all will be invited, but will everyone answer the call?

CHAPTER TWO

A Wedding Feast in the Kingdom of God

In the previous chapter, we looked at Old Testament texts that spoke of God's relationship to Abraham and Sarah and their offspring as one of mutual hospitality. It began with the account of Abraham's hospitality in serving a feast for his divine visitors and culminated with God's promised hospitality toward all humankind expressed in the image of a rich, delectable feast of fine food and wine.

Along with the promises of a great feast that are found in Isaiah, there are also the intimate descriptions of the relationship God seeks to bring about with Israel. Even though the people, in their exile from the Promised Land, feel themselves to be like widows, God will once again court them and be united with them as a husband is united to his wife.

Like a Groom Seeking a Bride, God Courts His People

Isaiah 54:4-8

> ⁴Do not fear, you shall not be put to shame;
>> do not be discouraged, you shall not be disgraced.
> For the shame of your youth you shall forget,
>> the reproach of your widowhood no longer remember.
> ⁵For your husband is your Maker;
>> the LORD of hosts is his name,
> Your redeemer, the Holy One of Israel,
>> called God of all the earth.

⁶The Lᴏʀᴅ calls you back,
   ᐟ like a wife forsaken and grieved in spirit,
A wife married in youth and then cast off,
   says your God.
⁷For a brief moment I abandoned you,
   but with great tenderness I will take you back.
⁸In an outburst of wrath, for a moment
   I hid my face from you;
But with enduring love I take pity on you,
   says the Lᴏʀᴅ, your redeemer.

These five verses in Isaiah 54 poignantly capture the deep sense of rejection felt by God's people during their exile in Babylon in the sixth century BC. It is the rejection a wife might feel in a time and culture when a wife was absolutely dependent on a husband's protection and provision. Just as the people of Judah have been driven from their homeland and forced to live by their wits, so a wife's rejection by her husband would find her without a home or any means to support herself. In these verses God, speaking through the prophet, admits his rejection of his people, his bride. He acknowledges their deep pain at his rejection. God tells them, "Do not fear," a reassurance, along with "have no fear," that is found eighty-two times in the New American Bible, Revised Edition (NABRE). When spoken by God, it is a reminder to readers of the Bible that the presence of God can indeed strike profound fear in our hearts, but that God's presence is, more importantly, one that we are to take hope in, rather than fear.

As a forsaken wife, the people of Judah have experienced deep "shame" and "reproach." They have been "forsaken," "grieved in spirit," and "abandoned." They have received from God "an outburst of wrath," and God has hidden his face from them. But they are no longer to be discouraged, for God is not just a husband to them; the Lord is their maker. This means that God is not just the creator of human life, but the people's reality as a people, as Judah, is God's doing and so the good news is that their identity as God's people, as God's beloved spouse, is to be restored.

Isaiah 62:5

For as a young man marries a virgin,
   your Builder shall marry you;
And as a bridegroom rejoices in his bride
   so shall your God rejoice in you.

Isaiah 62:5 has a similar characterization of Judah as God's beloved spouse, but with an important difference. Here there is no mention of a former relationship. Judah is not a spouse that has been abandoned and God is not a husband who has rejected her. Instead, God is like a young man, a new bridegroom, and Judah is like a virgin. Their union as husband and wife is, in this passage, a new relationship. It is not the joy of a once shamed wife being restored to honor; it is the joy of a new bride being rejoiced in by her bridegroom. We should think of a honeymoon rather than a reconciliation.

God is not just any wooer. This vision of God entering into marriage with a bride would carry with it images drawn from the most elaborate weddings experienced in the culture. God is the great and glorious king of heaven, and just as kings do not get married without throwing a great and elaborate feast in celebration, God would surely throw a feast without parallel in history. In the imagination of many, the expectation of a great and wonderful feast and the assurance that God intended, at some point in the future, to become the bridegroom of his chosen people was combined with the expectation that the Davidic throne would be re-established by a messiah. Thus the time of the messiah was thought by many to be the time when God's people would be called to the greatest wedding feast of all time.

There are other Old Testament passages that speak of God's relationship to the people of the covenant as a marital relationship (see Jer 2:2; Ezek 16:8; Hos 2:21).

Bruce Malina, in *The New Testament World,* provides an excellent analysis of just what it meant to be a married man or a married woman in patriarchal times, during the period of the monarchy, after the Babylonian exile and in the first century AD. Marriage practices among the people of the covenant developed and changed over time, but the wedding ceremony itself did not undergo radical changes. Marriages began with a binding betrothal, usually negotiated between the bridegroom's family and the family of the bride. A man and a woman did not simply fall in love and promise themselves to each other. Marriages were always about the honor and standing of the families involved.

Daughters lived very sheltered, protected lives and even at the time of the betrothal, the bridegroom and the future bride would have no contact with each other prior to the actual wedding.

The wedding ceremony would begin at the bride's home, from where she would be escorted by an entourage (the ten virgins of Jesus' parable in Matthew 25:1-13) to the home of the bridegroom. Once the bride was accepted into the home of the bridegroom, all would know that the marriage was to be considered consummated. The consummation would be quickly followed by as lavish feasting as could be afforded, feasting that could last for a number of days.

Throughout biblical times, families were "patrilineal," that is, they were headed by the male patriarch (the oldest living father in a family of however many generations) and families would trace their lineage directly from son to father to his father and so on, as evidenced by the many genealogies in the Bible. This is what makes Matthew's genealogy of Jesus so interesting as it makes special mention of four women in his lineage (Tamar, Rahab, Ruth, and Mary; see Matt 1:1-17). Why is all of this so important to our study of the Eucharist? The gospels tell us that when Jesus began his ministry he did so as a "bridegroom" and when he ate with sinners those meals were, by implication, the meals of a wedding feast. At the very least, they were the celebratory meals of a bridegroom and his friends in immediate anticipation of the wedding itself.

To assert that Jesus was the bridegroom God had sent to espouse his people was also to assert that the bride was due to enter the house of the Father. This could mean no less than what Jesus himself proclaimed at the beginning of his ministry: "This is the time of fulfillment. The kingdom of God is at hand. Repent, and believe in the gospel" (Mark 1:15).

As we shall see, dining with Jesus as the anticipation of the wedding feast that inaugurates the kingdom of God is something most clearly presented in the Synoptic Gospels and in Luke in particular. The theme of the wedding feast, however, also plays a very important role in John's gospel.

The Wedding in Cana

John 2:1-11

> [1]On the third day there was a wedding in Cana in Galilee, and the mother of Jesus was there. [2]Jesus and his disciples were also invited to the wedding. [3]When the wine ran short, the mother of Jesus said to him, "They have no wine." [4][And] Jesus said to her, "Woman, how does your concern affect me? My hour has not yet come." [5]His mother said to the servers, "Do whatever he tells you." [6]Now there were six stone water jars there for Jewish ceremonial washings, each holding twenty to thirty gallons. [7]Jesus told them, "Fill the jars with water." So they filled them to the brim. [8]Then he told them, "Draw some out now and take it to the headwaiter." So they took it. [9]And when the

headwaiter tasted the water that had become wine, without knowing where it came from (although the servers who had drawn the water knew), the headwaiter called the bridegroom [10]and said to him, "Everyone serves good wine first, and then when people have drunk freely, an inferior one; but you have kept the good wine until now." [11]Jesus did this as the beginning of his signs in Cana in Galilee and so revealed his glory, and his disciples began to believe in him.

That the miracle at Cana occurred on the third day is surely significant or it wouldn't be mentioned. Many commentators see it as a deliberate allusion to the resurrection. It is the first "sign" by which Jesus begins to reveal his "glory" (2:11), a glory that will be fully revealed in his passion and resurrection. Jesus' passion and resurrection are nowhere more intimately linked than in the Gospel of John. Francis Moloney, a prominent Johannine scholar, sees the importance of the third day as an allusion to God's self-revelation on Mt. Sinai on the third day (Exod 19:16). Likewise, Jesus, whose glory is "the glory as of the Father's only Son" (John 1:14), begins to reveal his glory at Cana "on the third day."

As a footnote to John 2:6 in the NABRE indicates, Old Testament prophets assured Israel that in the last days God would bless them with abundance. Mountains dripping with the juice of grapes is a potent sign of that abundance in Amos 9:13-14. In Hosea 14:8 Israel's renown will be like the wine of Lebanon, and Jeremiah 31:12 says that all Israel "shall come streaming to the LORD's blessings: / The grain, the wine, and the oil, / flocks of sheep and cattle."

Many have focused on Mary's presence at Cana and the surprisingly curt way in which Jesus responds to his mother. It has been noted that calling a woman "woman" is neither unusual nor rude in Jesus' time or culture, but also that there is no record of anyone in that time and place ever speaking to one's mother and calling her woman. What John has probably recorded here ("Woman, how does your concern affect me? My hour has not yet come") is another example, like those found in Matthew (12:47-50) and Mark (3:31-35), of Jesus pointedly rooting his ministry to Israel in his call from the Father and that he is in no way beholden to purely family interests. Nevertheless, Jesus acts in a way that truly responds to Mary's concern that the host has run out of wine.

At first, Jesus seems to reject Mary's request because his "hour" has not yet come, but in changing the water to wine, we learn that hour must surely be approaching. In John 17:1 Jesus will ask the Father to glorify him, because his hour has come. Jesus' glory is first revealed to his disciples in the changing of water to wine at a wedding, and the wine Jesus has brought forth is better than what has been previously experienced. We can be sure that this later wine that Jesus gives has far greater meaning than a party favor at a wedding between just one couple in Cana some two thousand years ago. This wine reveals the glory of God's only-begotten Son.

The late Raymond Brown, perhaps the most noted scholar of the Gospel of John in modern times, tells us that this discovery of better wine at a late time during a wedding feast is a proclamation that the messianic age has begun for Israel.

Shortly after the account of the wedding at Cana, John once again employs a wedding motif in relation to Jesus' ministry (John 3:23-29). When John the Baptist's disciples question him, with implied concern over Jesus' rising popularity, he reminds them that he is not the Messiah, and immediately begins referring to the one who is the Messiah (and by direct implication, a reference to Jesus as the Messiah) as the bridegroom. John the Baptist is merely the best man.

John Calls Jesus the Bridegroom

John 3:25-30

> [25]Now a dispute arose between the disciples of John and a Jew about ceremonial washings. [26]So they came to John and said to him, "Rabbi, the one who was with you across the Jordan, to whom you testified, here he is baptizing and everyone is coming to him." [27]John answered and said, "No one can receive anything except what has been given him from heaven. [28]You yourselves can testify that I said [that] I am not the Messiah, but that I was sent before him. [29]The one who has the bride is the bridegroom; the best man, who stands and listens to him, rejoices greatly at the bridegroom's voice. So this joy of mine has been made complete. [30]He must increase; I must decrease."

The message John the Baptist sends in the Gospel of John is clear: the promise of a marriage between God and God's people is being fulfilled by Jesus. The depiction of the people of God as the betrothed of God in Christ appears outside the gospels as well. After the resurrection, the message of Jesus' gospel of the kingdom becomes centered on Jesus as the risen Lord in that kingdom. His followers will come to understand themselves as messianic people, a people called out of Israel and the Gentile nations to be a new people. This new people, this "church" (*ekklesia*), will be described in Ephesians (5:25-32) and the book of Revelation (19:6-9; 21:2-4, 9-10) as the bride of Christ.

Jesus as the bridegroom in the forthcoming marriage between God and his people is prevalent in the Synoptic Gospels as well. Matthew also records a connection between Jesus and John the Baptist that focuses on Jesus as the bridegroom. In Matthew 9:14-15, John the Baptist's disciples come to Jesus with a concern about a particular difference between them and Jesus' disciples. John's disciples fast, Jesus' disciples don't. They ask Jesus directly for a reason: "Then the disciples of John approached him and said, 'Why do we and the Pharisees fast [much], but your disciples do not fast?' Jesus answered them, 'Can the wedding guests mourn as long as the bridegroom is with them? The days will come when the bridegroom is taken away from them, and then they will fast.'" Mark 2:19-20 and Luke 5:34-35 provide parallel accounts of this.

A meal enjoyed in Jesus' presence is a meal with the bridegroom. This does not mean that every meal with Jesus is the same as the wedding feast, but they certainly anticipate it. A modern analogy might be to say that these meals with Jesus were like participating in the bridegroom's rehearsal dinner. These meals mirror the "now, but not yet" nature of the kingdom of God Jesus proclaimed. Jesus announced that the kingdom of God is very near, that it is "at hand" (Mark 1:15), but it is also something that must be sought after above and beyond any material good: "So do not worry and say, 'What are we to eat?' or 'What are we to drink?' or 'What are we to wear?' All these things the pagans seek. Your heavenly Father knows that you need them all. But seek first the kingdom [of God] and his righteousness, and all these things will be given you besides" (Matt 6:31-33). Jesus' good news is that the kingdom can be experienced in his company, so while his followers still have him with them they have no need to fast, but the wedding feast that symbolizes the fullness of the kingdom is yet to come. A time is also coming when the bridegroom's disciples will need to fast.

The prospect of the bridegroom being taken away does not mean the wedding feast is not going to take place. The foretaste of that feast that those who dine with him enjoy during his ministry is also an invitation to prepare themselves for the ultimate feast, a feast that is also synonymous with being "saved." Eating and drinking with Jesus does not guarantee one will dine in that ultimate feast.

Dining with Jesus Does Not Guarantee Salvation

Luke 13:23-30

> [23]Someone asked him, "Lord, will only a few people be saved?"
> He answered them, [24]"Strive to enter through the narrow door, for

many, I tell you, will attempt to enter but will not be strong enough. [25]After the master of the house has arisen and locked the door, then will you stand outside knocking and saying, 'Lord, open the door for us.' He will say to you in reply, 'I do not know where you are from.' [26]And you will say, 'We ate and drank in your company and you taught in our streets.' [27]Then he will say to you, 'I do not know where [you] are from. Depart from me, all you evildoers!' [28]And there will be wailing and grinding of teeth when you see Abraham, Isaac, and Jacob and all the prophets in the kingdom of God and you yourselves cast out. [29]And people will come from the east and the west and from the north and the south and will recline at table in the kingdom of God. [30]For behold, some are last who will be first, and some are first who will be last."

How widespread was the expectation of an actual feast being part of the messianic kingdom during the late second temple period (the time within which Jesus' ministry occurred)? This is debated, but there is no doubt that within our four canonical gospels, eating and drinking with Jesus reveals this messianic expectation in a surprising and controversial way.

In Luke the invitation to a great feast appears as a parable with dire implications for those who refuse the invitation (14:15-24). In Matthew Jesus tells a similar parable concerning the nature of the kingdom of heaven, which he compares to a king's invitation to a wedding feast for his son. This feast is of such great importance that not only those who reject the invitation are punished, but those who would presume to attend it in improper attire will lose their life (Matt 22:2-14).

In the Synoptic Gospels, and in Luke in particular, Jesus' ministry often involves eating and drinking with sinners. This is at the heart of some criticisms of Jesus. The Pharisees complain about Jesus dining with sinners in Matthew 9:10-11, in Mark 2:15-16, and several times in Luke (5:30; 7:36-50; 15:2; 19:7).

The irony of their complaint against Jesus is that Luke provides two lengthy accounts of Jesus being invited into the home of a Pharisee. During the course of those meals it becomes obvious that Jesus is still eating with sinners, but the sinners he is dining with are Pharisees (7:36-50; 11:37-44). In *A Body Broken for a Broken People*, Francis Moloney, SDB, examines the meals Jesus eats in all the gospels (as well as the Eucharist throughout the New Testament) and stresses that meals with Jesus, including the Eucharist, are meals intended for sinners. The mistake of the Pharisees is the greatest mistake of all: to eat with Jesus and not to be aware of one's sinfulness.

This seems very much in line with what Pope Francis stressed during a general audience on February 12, 2014: "If any one of us does not feel in need of the mercy of God, does not see himself as a sinner, it is better for him not to go to Mass! We go to Mass because we are sinners and we want to receive God's pardon, to participate in the redemption of Jesus, in his forgiveness."

This leads us to a special theme in Luke. Eugene LaVerdiere, in *The Breaking of the Bread*, discusses at length just how important meals with Jesus are to Luke's gospel. There are ten meals with Jesus in Luke and they punctuate the gospel in such a way that it can be said that everything Jesus does in Luke happens either before or after a meal. Most of us are fortunate enough to eat three square meals a day, but it is doubtful that we would tell the story of our lives around the ten most important meals we ever ate. Luke, however, provides us with his account of the life and mission of Christ framed by ten all-important meals.

Robert Karris, OFM, in the often amusing, always enlightening *Eating Your Way Through Luke's Gospel*, also reminds us that Jesus consistently ate with known public sinners and just how serious this scandalous behavior was considered by the Pharisees. Jesus' way of eating is the reason why he was killed, Karris claims, with more than ample evidence for his claim.

Eating in the presence of Christ is all-important for Luke, for doing so culminates in that ultimate fellowship with Jesus in the Eucharist. As Jesus tells the Pharisees in Luke 5:32, "I have not come to call the righteous to repentance but sinners."

The Multiplication of the Loaves

Jesus' miraculous feeding of the multitudes has much to tell us about the Eucharist in the early church. At least one account of Jesus feeding thousands of people from a meager supply of food is present in all four gospels. Scholars and students alike have pondered the similarities between the two accounts found in both Matthew (14:15-21; 15:29-38) and Mark (6:31-44; 8:1-9) of Jesus' feeding of a multitude. On the surface they are so similar that many have speculated that oral tradition may have preserved the memory of a single event in two slightly different ways. Those who favor this possibility are quick to note that both Luke and John record Jesus feeding a multitude of five thousand by the Sea of Galilee but make no mention of a second event of a feeding of four thousand (see Luke 9:10-17 and John 6:1-15). This theory finds additional support in the strong likelihood that Luke had access to Mark's gospel but chose to omit the second feeding in his gospel. It could be speculated that Luke did so because of his professed interest in historical accuracy (see Luke 1:1-4).

In this study, where the focus is on the biblical roots and themes related to the Eucharist, it is not necessary to make historical judgments concerning the two feedings found in Matthew and Mark. Instead we will take the lead provided by the late Eugene LaVerdiere, and investigate the theological importance of the differences between the two miraculous feedings as found in Mark. It is widely accepted that Mark's account of the two feedings was the original source for Matthew's account of the same. Even if what is called "Markan priority" were to be disputed, LaVerdiere's research would still reveal a rich strain of theological development that distinguishes the two different feedings as recorded in Mark.

LaVerdiere devoted much of his research to exploring the myriad, intricate connections to the Eucharist found throughout the gospels, the book of Acts, and Paul's letters to the Galatians and Second Corinthians. Beyond the accounts specifically devoted to the Lord's Supper, LaVerdiere was insistent that every meal taken in the presence of Christ between his baptism and his ascension was cast by the evangelists as "eucharistic," even when they were not in fact a celebration of Eucharist itself. LaVerdiere stresses that any meal where Jesus took bread, blessed God, broke the bread, and shared the meal with others was an incomparable feast partaken in the real presence of Christ. As the root meaning of the word "Eucharist" is "to give thanks," any of those meals would have had eucharistic overtones.

LaVerdiere was adept at uncovering the nuances by which each evangelist applied the authentic traditions of Jesus' deeds and teachings to address the needs and concerns for the local Christian communities to which they were writing. This is not far afield from what a skilled homilist will do today in breaking open Scripture to meet the needs of a particular assembly. LaVerdiere's careful analysis of the two feedings in Mark's account helps us to see the eucharistic overtones of both accounts while also revealing some remarkable details concerning the growth of the early church and its inclusion of all men and women, including children, in its eucharistic celebrations.

We place the two accounts side by side to make them easier to compare, noting some of the significant differences between the accounts in a table so it will be easier to refer back to them when they are discussed:

Mark 6:31-45

[31]He [Jesus] said to them, "Come away by yourselves to a deserted place and rest a while." People were coming and going in great numbers, and they had no opportunity even to eat. [32]So they went off in the boat by themselves to a deserted place. [33]People saw them leaving and many came to know about it. They hastened there on foot from all the towns and arrived at the place before them. . . .

[34]When he disembarked and saw the vast crowd, his heart was moved with pity for them, for they were like sheep without a shepherd; and he began to teach them many things. [35]By now it was already late and his disciples approached him and said, "This is a deserted place and it is already very late. [36]Dismiss them so that they can go to the surrounding farms and villages and buy themselves something to eat." [37]He said to them in reply, "Give them some food yourselves." But they said to him, "Are we to buy two hundred days' wages worth of food and give it to them to eat?" [38]He asked them, "How many loaves do you have? Go and see." And when they had found out they said, "Five loaves and two fish." [39]So he gave orders to have them sit down in groups on the green grass. [40]The people took their places in rows by hundreds and by fifties. [41]Then, taking the five loaves and the two fish and looking up to heaven, he said the blessing, broke the loaves, and gave them to [his] disciples to set before the people; he also divided the two fish among them all. [42]They all ate and were satisfied. [43]And they picked up twelve wicker baskets full of fragments and what was left of the fish. [44]Those who ate [of the loaves] were five thousand men. . . .

[45]Then he made his disciples get into the boat and precede him to the other side toward Bethsaida, while he dismissed the crowd.

Mark 7:31

Again he left the district of Tyre and went by way of Sidon to the Sea of Galilee, into the district of the Decapolis.

Mark 8:1-9a

[1]In those days when there again was a great crowd without anything to eat, he summoned the disciples and said, [2]"My heart is moved with pity for the crowd, because they have been with me now for three days and have nothing to eat. [3]If I send them away hungry to their homes, they will collapse on the way, and some of them have come a great distance." [4]His disciples answered him, "Where can anyone get enough bread to satisfy them here in this deserted place?" [5]Still he asked them, "How many loaves do you have?" "Seven," they replied. [6]He ordered the crowd to sit down on the ground. Then, taking the seven loaves he gave thanks, broke them, and gave them to his disciples to distribute, and they distributed them to the crowd. [7]They also had a few fish. He said the blessing over them and ordered them distributed also. [8]They ate and were satisfied. They picked up the fragments left over—seven baskets. [9]There were about four thousand people.

	Mark 6:31-45	Mark 8:1-9a
Location	Western shore of Galilee	Eastern shore of Galilee (7:31)
Demographics	Jewish	Gentile
Jesus' motivation	The people need a shepherd (see Num 27:17)	Pity on the people's hunger
Food source	Five loaves, two fish	Seven loaves and a few fish
Grouping	Hundreds and fifties on green grass (Ps 23; Ezek 34)	
Blessing	"Looking up to heaven, he said the blessing, broke the loaves" (Jewish blessing of God)	He gave thanks, broke them "*They also had a few fish.* He said the blessing over them and ordered them distributed also." (Gentile blessing of the food)
Distribution	Given to the disciples to distribute	Given to the disciples to distribute
Response	"They all ate and were satisfied."	"They ate and were satisfied."
Leftovers	Twelve baskets of fragments and fish *Kophinoi (Jewish style baskets)*	Seven baskets of fragments *Spurides (Gentile style baskets)*
Number and gender	Five thousand men	Four thousand people
Lessons taught	On the Jewish side Jesus teaches new rules concerning purity and food laws	On the Gentile side he teaches the disciples that the Gentiles must also participate in the mission

The first account in Mark of Jesus feeding a multitude has deep resonances with four Old Testament readings. In 6:34, we are told, "When he disembarked and saw the vast crowd, his heart was moved with pity for them, for they were like sheep without a shepherd." This concern for the shepherdless is an echo of Numbers 27:16-17, where Moses prays, "May the LORD, the God of the spirits of all humanity, set over the community someone who will be their leader in battle and who will lead them out and bring them in, that the LORD's community may not be like sheep without a shepherd." In Ezekiel 34:15, God promises that the day will come when the Lord will become the shepherd of his people.

When Jesus has the people arranged in groups of hundreds and fifties, it recalls the arrangement of the Israelites in their wilderness pilgrimage during the exodus (Exod 18:21-25). There is an almost peculiar note in 6:39 that these groups of hundreds and fifties are seated "on the green grass." The presence of grass has not been noted prior to this, setting up the entire account as a reflection of Psalm 23, where God is the shepherd who gives the psalmist rest in green pastures and sets a table for him to feast without fear from enemies.

When Mark wrote his gospel, perhaps just before AD 70, he was not writing what we today would call a biography. Good biographies necessarily attend to a great many historical details that are left out of Mark. For example, Mark tells us nothing about Jesus' life before his baptism in the Jordan by John. But the gospel we call Mark is something far more important to Christians than a biography would be. Because Mark is a gospel, and not a biography, it has as its intention the task of presenting us with the person of Jesus and what it means for us to acknowledge that Jesus is the Christ (the Messiah) and the Son of God. Mark wanted the Christian community that was the first to hear his gospel proclaimed (very few would actually be able to read it) to accept the challenge Jesus posed to his first disciples, the apostles: "Whoever wishes to come after me must deny himself, take up his cross, and follow me. For whoever wishes to save his life will lose it, but whoever loses his life for my sake and that of the gospel will save it" (8:34-35).

Mark presented those early Christians with a living Jesus, the risen one, whom they believed was their source of salvation. Mark knew these fellow Christians believed that Jesus was present to them in their eucharistic celebrations. His gospel depiction of Jesus would have continuously challenged them to accept their calling to follow Jesus to the cross, as it ought ourselves as well. We, however, often read the gospels as though they were biographies focused entirely on accurately depicting persons engaged in events just as they happened in the time and place that they occurred. As a gospel, however, Mark deliberately portrayed Jesus as the Messiah committed to leading Mark's community to salvation. Mark recorded what Jesus said and did, but he made certain that his community would be directly addressed, in their time and place, by the Jesus they fellowshipped with in their eucharistic celebrations.

It would help us to appreciate Mark's telling of the two feedings of the multitudes if we approached them from the viewpoint of the early Christians who first heard it. While immersing ourselves into their world and mindsets would take a great deal of study, we can make note of a few essentials that will help us in our reading. If we were Mark's community, most of us would be illiterate and even those of us who could read would have to depend on hearing the gospel proclaimed because there were no printing presses to make extra copies of Mark available.

Making Mark available to other Christian communities would involve a lot of time and effort in diligently copying it word for word by hand. This means that we would be experiencing the proclamation of Mark's gospel as a communal event. Our communal experience would be one of engagement with the person of Jesus as the gospel presents him to us, not as someone acting in the past, but as the Christ who comes to us in our time and place in order to lead us to salvation. Indeed, the proclamation of the gospel and the homily that follows should serve the same function in our own eucharistic celebrations.

Also, Mark's community would never have heard "the gospel" quite like this before. They would have heard the basic truths of the gospel (the *kerygma*)—that Jesus is the Christ; that he walked among his people, curing their illnesses, eating and drinking with sinners, teaching all who would listen about God's love; and that he was tragically crucified by the authorities, died, and rose to new life on the third day. They would have never, however, heard anyone put Jesus' deeds and teachings into a single, consecutive narrative before. Hearing Mark's gospel for the first time, it would be as though they were being plunged into the story, as this story is not just telling them who Jesus is, but it is Jesus telling them who they are.

Finally, as Mark's community, they would know how things have gone with the faith since Jesus rose from the dead. Jesus was a Jew, he ministered to primarily Jewish people throughout his ministry, and yet most of Mark's community are Gentiles and they have many questions about how their Jewish Messiah came to be our Savior. This transition of Christian faith from being primarily an expression of Jewish messianic faith to a chiefly Gentile religion had caused great turmoil among believers (see Acts 15:1-2; Gal 1:1–2:10).

The faith of Mark's community would be tangible in their own lived experience of forgiveness through baptism and in their sense of communion with Christ and each other through their celebration of Eucharist, for which they would gather together in someone's home every Sunday. It was in the sharing of Eucharist that their identity as Jesus' flock, a people he shepherded as they anxiously awaited his return, would have been reaffirmed over and over again. Their anxiousness for his return would be all the more palatable because some were experiencing persecution in various forms.

When they heard about the feeding of the multitude on the western shore of Galilee (Mark 6:31-45), they may well have heard some of the details before, as it may have been recounted by a number of teachers.

The details, however, might be a little fuzzy in the community's mind for having been told by different teachers who agreed on the main points but sometimes differed because of the existence of different channels of oral tradition. And so when they heard Mark tell of two separate feedings of different crowds in two different places, this may be the first time they became aware that there were two different feedings. But whether or not there actually were two different feedings, when they heard what makes the two feedings different, they would have smiled with understanding, because it was telling them their own story, the story of how the gospel grew out of a Jewish setting and went into a Gentile setting.

When these early Christians heard the accounts of Jesus feeding the multitudes, they did so in the context of their own eucharistic fellowship with Jesus. Furthermore, Mark's depiction of both accounts was deliberately honed to bring instruction to those responsible for shepherding and nurturing the local church. They would be the ones identifying themselves with Jesus' first disciples, and would see the way Jesus tasked those first disciples with feeding those who came out to be healed and instructed by Jesus as instruction for them in their care of Jesus' flock. "Give them some food yourselves," he tells them in the first feeding account (Mark 6:37).

In both feedings it is Jesus who pronounces the blessing, but in the first account he does so in Jewish fashion, that is, he utters a blessing of God in thanksgiving for the bread and not a blessing of the food itself (6:41). In the second account, however, Jesus offers a blessing of the fish, which would be common among Gentiles (8:7). In both accounts the food is given to the disciples to distribute to the people. This is the all-important message concerning the Eucharist in the two accounts: Jesus' ministry has become the ministerial task of his disciples.

The most important difference between the two accounts is in their location. The first feeding takes place on the western shore of the Galilee, which was a predominately Jewish region. Between the two feedings, Mark prepares those who listen to his gospel for a great shift in Jesus' ministry. Jesus does away with Jewish dietary regulations. His followers are allowed to eat without first performing the traditional washing of hands, which was a religious duty, not a health concern (7:1-4). He also, in effect, declares all food "clean," vacating the entire corpus of Torah regulations forbidding the eating of a large number of foods (7:17-20). This declaration is a Markan interpretation of Jesus' teaching, which is why most translations put 7:19b in parenthesis. Jesus' teaching—that a person is defiled by what comes from within, not what goes into the person—is also included in Matthew's gospel (15:15-20), but the Markan assertion that this means Jesus declared all foods clean is not mentioned in Matthew. Luke does not mention this teaching at all. In fact, the laying aside of dietary regulations is not recorded by Luke until after the resurrection, in the book of Acts (10:1-49; 15:19-20), when Peter receives a vision from God prior to visiting and baptizing a Gentile named Cornelius.

After Mark portrays Jesus as voiding ritual food laws, we are told that Jesus and his disciples travel into Gentile territory (7:24-30). There, they encounter a Gentile woman who asks Jesus to cast a demon from her daughter. Jesus responds, "Let the children be fed first. For it is not right to take the food of the children and throw it to the dogs" (v. 27). To our ears, this caricature of Gentiles as "dogs" (an unclean animal) is far from politically correct language. The woman, however, makes a counterpoint to Jesus' assertion, saying, "Lord, even the dogs under the table eat the children's scraps" (v. 28). Scholars have noted that in the honor and shame society in which the gospels are set, where losing an argument is always a shameful thing, this is the only account of a verbal dispute that Jesus loses. He acknowledges his defeat by healing her daughter: "For saying this, you may go. The demon has gone out of your daughter" (v. 29). If Mark's audience is not yet fully aware that Jesus knew the time would come that his disciples would take his gospel to the Gentiles, the second account of feeding a multitude would make it an absolute certainty.

That the first account describes Jesus feeding five thousand "men" while the second account tells of Jesus feeding four thousand "people" is something LaVerdiere also claims shows an important theological development in eucharistic practice. As Jesus' ministry was to continue in the care of his disciples after the resurrection, it grew from being almost exclusively directed toward Jews to one that found its ultimate success among Gentiles. LaVerdiere asserts that early celebrations of Eucharist among Jewish followers of the risen Jesus may not have included women. If not exclusively male, other scholars do wonder if they were segregated by gender, as meals were among Jews at that time. We know from Paul's discussion of the Corinthians' eucharistic celebrations that Gentile men and women gathered together for Eucharist (e.g., 1 Cor 11:3-10).

CHAPTER THREE

The Last Supper

In the previous chapters our focus was on meals with Jesus, some of them miraculous, all of them special and "eucharistic" without actually being Eucharist because they were meals in which Jesus was physically present to those who dined with him. There was a theme to many of those meals—they were marriage feasts, meals with Jesus, the bridegroom, in expectation of the great marriage between God and his people that inaugurates the kingdom of God.

We concluded the previous chapter by examining how the second feeding of the multitude in Mark 8 was presented by Mark to his community in such a way that it would speak to them of their own inclusion, as "people"—Gentile men, women, and children—in that miraculous feeding because of their fellowship with Christ and each other in the Eucharist.

In this chapter, we will explore in detail the Last Supper of Our Lord as presented in each of the Synoptic Gospels, but we will do so by beginning where we left off, because the events and encounters of Mark 8:9b-33 provide a poignant bridge between the kingdom inaugurating wedding feast and the Last Supper. After dismissing the crowds he has just fed, Jesus and his disciples travel by boat to Dalmanutha (a place for which there is as yet no archaeological record, but Matthew 15:39 refers instead to Magadan, which may have been the home of Mary Magdalene). There he encounters some Pharisees who demand a sign from heaven. Jesus refuses, but their demand is part of a thematic strain that flows through the rest of Mark 8. There are claims being made about

Jesus' identity, and the Pharisees are testing Jesus to see if the stories of his special powers are true.

Back on the boat, Jesus warns his disciples against the leaven of the Pharisees. Leaven, in this case, is a symbol of a pervasive evil that has infected the Pharisees' attitude toward Jesus. Their demand for proof is born out of doubt, out of a desire to reject Jesus and his ministry. The disciples misunderstand Jesus, which is a pervasive theme throughout Mark's gospel. They think Jesus' warning against leaven has something to do with their only having one loaf of bread with them. Jesus asks them how they can be worried about bread after just witnessing two different feedings of the multitude. They do not understand Jesus or his mission yet, and the rest of Mark 8 is going to drive this point home.

One of the strangest accounts of Jesus performing a healing appears in Mark 8:22-26, where Jesus has to make two attempts to heal a blind man on their way to Caesarea Philippi: "When they arrived at Bethsaida, they brought to him a blind man and begged him to touch him. He took the blind man by the hand and led him outside the village. Putting spittle on his eyes he laid his hands on him and asked, 'Do you see anything?' Looking up he replied, 'I see people looking like trees and walking.' Then he laid hands on his eyes a second time and he saw clearly; his sight was restored and he could see everything distinctly. Then he sent him home and said, 'Do not even go into the village.'"

Why would Jesus need to make two attempts at healing this man?

Many scholars today agree that Mark has included this account of Jesus having to make two attempts to heal a blind man as part of a typical Markan pattern, called a "Markan sandwich," in which an apparent interruption in the narrative is actually illustrating a theme. The interruption is actually the meat of the sandwich. In Mark 8, the prevailing theme is the disciples' failure to understand Jesus and what it means to be the Messiah. Jesus knows that being identified as the Messiah will lead to his execution, but as the Messiah there are things he must still accomplish before he is put to death. For this reason Jesus cautions those he heals against proclaiming his good deeds or calling him the Messiah. His disciples, however, refuse to accept that Jesus, because he is the Messiah, will be put to death by the authorities.

In Mark 8:27-30, Jesus asks his disciples who the people are saying he is, to which there is a number of responses, everything from John the Baptist to Elijah or even one of the prophets. "But who do you say that I am?" Jesus asks, and Peter volunteers his famous reply, "You are the Messiah" (v. 29). Jesus' response to Peter has long troubled Christians who assume Jesus would want Peter and everyone to have faith in him: "Then he [Jesus] warned them not to tell anyone about him" (v. 30). The disciples, however, have failed to "see" who Jesus really is. They may have been quick to drop their fishing nets or tax collections to follow Jesus, but, just like the blind man who can only see blurred images after first being touched by Jesus, the disciples will also need a renewed effort from Jesus if they are ever to understand what it is to follow this Messiah.

In Mark 2:19-20 we learn that Jesus' disciples do not fast because they are with the bridegroom. The impossibility of fasting in the bridegroom's presence is made doubly clear in Mark with the two feedings of throngs of thousands from the most meagre portions available. The disciples are enjoying the prospect of the ultimate messianic feast. But then, after the second feeding of a multitude, Mark 8 proceeds with Jesus teaching them what lies ahead not just for himself, but for anyone who follows Jesus. All who wish to follow Jesus must be willing to lose their lives in order to enter the kingdom the Messiah will establish. For Jesus' first disciples the wedding feast with the bridegroom will eventually take on the most somber of meanings at a final meal with Jesus. What Mark tells us about them, he is clearly telling his own community as they anticipate the kingdom of God in their eucharistic celebrations.

The inability of Jesus' disciples to accept that Jesus must die in order to complete his mission, and that they themselves will have to take up their own crosses in order to be his followers, comes to a head in the Synoptic Gospels on the night he was betrayed and his subsequent crucifixion. Jesus, however, made certain that they would never forget his pending sacrifice in a meal forever remembered as the Last Supper, a meal that will always be an essential part of the church's life, celebrated in remembrance of him as the Lord's Supper, our Eucharist.

Cultural and Religious Context of the Last Supper

The Last Supper's religious significance to sacramental Christians is unparalleled, but it was also a meal eaten between Jews within a thoroughly Jewish religious context, whether or not it was a Passover meal.

According to Jerome Kodell in *The Eucharist in the New Testament*, Jewish family meals in the first century were never secular gatherings. Eating together as a family was always a religious event. Sharing a meal with guests was also, in and of itself, a religious event that bound the partakers together in a sacred bond known as a "covenant of salt." Numbers 18:19 and 2 Chronicles 13:5 speak respectively of God's covenant of salt with the children of Israel and with David and his heirs. Put simply, a covenant of salt was the bond that formed between people who shared a meal together, a covenant named for the essential spice that brings flavor and enjoyment to food and thus also to the relationship. It certainly must have bothered certain religious leaders that Jesus bound himself to known sinners in a covenant of salt.

Jewish family meals began with the head of the household holding bread in his hands while blessing God, then breaking the bread and distributing it among all gathered. The blessing, known as the *berakah*, was simple but profound: "Blessed are you, O Lord our God, King of the world, who brings forth bread from the earth." There is another formal blessing after the meal, the *Birkat HaMazon*. It is lengthier than the first blessing and it is based on the command in Deuteronomy 8:10: "But when you have eaten and are satisfied, you must bless the LORD, your God, for the good land he has given you." Typical family meals of the time would include only water as a beverage, but wine would be used on special occasions.

We have no texts from the time of Jesus that provide the specific details of festive Jewish meals, but literature describing them from within the first two centuries afterwards is believed to reflect the meals of Jesus' time as well. Guests would arrive at a home large enough for a host of some means to provide a festive meal and would be seated in a ground-floor anteroom on benches and chairs, awaiting the arrival of all the guests. Once the meal was ready to commence, servants would provide the guests with water to wash their right hands, which would be used for eating without utensils. Wine would be mixed with water and served along with hors d'oeuvres. Each guest would bless God for these before proceeding upstairs to the dining room, where they would recline at table. Reclining at table was a cultural adaptation made under Roman influence, even at Passover. Exodus 12:11 commanded that the Passover be eaten standing up, as though in a hurry to flee from Egypt.

Once reclining at table, guests would again wash their hands, but both hands now, as they awaited the main course. As in any family meal, the main course would begin with a signal from the host (head of the household), who would begin with a blessing of God, king of the world and creator of all, while holding bread that he would then break and distribute. Subsequent courses would be served in bowls; as each arrived at the table the host would again offer a blessing and then dip his hand in the bowl to serve himself, after which each guest would also retrieve a serving from the bowl.

Another cup of wine would be served with the main course(s). The host would bless this cup in the name of all attending, saying, "Blessed are you, O Lord, Our God, eternal king, who creates the fruit of the wine." Refills would be available, but for each refill, each guest would pronounce a private blessing.

The meal would conclude with dessert, which might consist of bread and salted foodstuffs, rather than sweets. The final blessing would then be said, and it was generally lengthy, including readings from Scripture. On very important occasions this final blessing would be recited over a final (third, with previous refills not being counted) cup of wine that would be passed around to all the guests. Kodell tells us that this special cup is the cup "after supper" that Luke and Paul identify as the cup of the new covenant in Jesus' blood. It is also the "cup of blessing" that Paul mentions in 1 Corinthians 10:16.

If the Last Supper was not a Passover meal (following John), then, as it is described in the Synoptic Gospels, it would have been a Jewish festive meal, which bears many similarities to the Passover—the most important of Jewish festive meals. If, however, it was a Passover meal (following the Synoptic Gospels), there would be some unique features that would have distinguished it from other festive meals.

The Celebration of the Passover Meal

The Passover meal was quite similar to the typical Jewish festival meal described above, but by the late first and early second century AD it had taken on some additional characteristics, some of which, including a fourth cup of wine, may not have been part of a typical Passover meal in Jesus' time.

One important distinction of the Passover meal is the menu. Each course has a prescribed foodstuff. A Passover meal is to begin with lettuce dipped in vinegar and salt water. While the blessings occur as during any festive meal, the main courses at Passover must include unleavened bread, bitter herbs, *haroseth* (which comprised nuts, fruit, and wine), as well as the paschal lamb (see Exod 12:1-5). Once the second cup of wine is prepared, according to ritual formula in a family celebration, the son would ask the father why this night is different from all other nights. The host would then ask what differences the son has noticed. The son would then respond with four distinctive aspects of the Passover meal:

1. On all other nights we eat leavened or unleavened bread. Tonight we eat only unleavened bread.

2. Every other night we eat all kinds of green vegetables. Tonight we eat only bitter herbs.

3. Every other night we eat meat either cooked, roasted, or stewed. Tonight we eat only roasted.

4. Every other night we dip once (bread into salt water). Tonight we dip twice.

The host (the father, if a family Passover) would answer these questions with the story of the Haggadah, the story of Israel's slavery in Egypt and God's miraculous, saving act of deliverance through the prophet Moses.

Festive Meal	Passover
First Course (Hors d'oeuvres) Washing of one hand 1st cup of wine with individual blessings Appetizers with individual blessings	*First Course* (Hors d'oeuvres) Washing of one hand 1st cup of wine with individual blessings *Blessing for the sanctification of the day* Appetizers with individual blessings
Main Course Washing of both hands Breaking of the bread with blessing by host 2nd cup of wine with blessing by host Sharing of meal	*Main Course* Washing of both hands Breaking of the bread with blessing by host 2nd cup of wine with blessing by host followed by questions from son to the host Sharing of meal *unleavened bread, paschal lamb*
Third Course (Dessert) Bread and salted foodstuffs Thanksgiving for meal (On occasion: 3rd cup of wine ["cup of blessing"] shared by guests)	*Questioning and Haggadah* *First part of the Hallel psalms* Thanksgiving for the meal *3rd cup of wine ("cup of blessing") shared by guests* *4th cup of wine and the 2nd part of the Hallel psalms*

* See Jerome Kodell, *The Eucharist in the New Testament*, ed. Mary Ann Getty, Zacchaeus Studies: New Testament Series (Wilmington, DE: Michael Glazier, 1988), 41–44.

In comparing the accounts of the Last Supper in Matthew, Mark, Luke, and First Corinthians and the manner in which they quote Jesus, it is important to remember that all four are reporting in Greek, while Aramaic would have been employed during the historic Last Supper. While insights might be gained into certain theological nuances of the four accounts based on each one's particular use of Greek, none of them are actually quoting Jesus. Instead, they are handing on traditions that have attempted to translate Jesus' words into another language.

What is most notable about all four accounts of the Last Supper is how few details of that meal are actually recorded in any of them. Jewish meals, especially festive meals like the Passover, had a prescribed menu and a prescribed order of serving each course and cup of wine, but these Last Supper accounts for the most part only focus on the eucharistic aspects of the meal. This tells us that the traditions behind the accounts of the Last Supper were handed on from within the liturgical practices of the various Christian communities responsible for them. From these Last Supper accounts we can hear distinct echoes of the eucharistic liturgies celebrated by early Christians.

We look at what all four accounts have in common as a way of appreciating the core of the tradition concerning the Last Supper, but in no way should this common core be construed as being more important or more authentic than material that may be unique to one source (Luke has the most unique material) or than that which appears in two or three accounts. Each account represents a strand of tradition and the presence of a common core can easily be seen as lending credence to each account. Later, we will examine the differences between the accounts in the hope of discovering what they add to the richness of our understanding of the Last Supper.

All four accounts tell us that Jesus took bread and said a blessing (or gave thanks), broke the bread, and said, "This is my body" (literally translated, simply "this my body"). Then, all four agree that he took a cup, saying that "this . . . is my blood" and that his blood constitutes a "covenant." In a short and simple list it would appear as thus:

1. Jesus took bread

2. He blessed (or gave thanks)

3. Jesus broke the bread

4. Jesus identified the bread as his body

5. Jesus took a cup

6. The cup is Jesus' covenantal blood

It is not said that the bread Jesus took was the unleavened bread (*matzos*) that would have been the only bread consumed at Passover, but in the Synoptic accounts, the association of this meal with the Passover makes that an implicit assumption. Using Jerome Kodell's *The Eucharist in the New Testament* as the valuable resource it is, there are several

The Accounts of the Last Supper in Matthew, Mark, Luke, and I Corinthians

Matthew 26:26-29	Mark 14:22-25	Luke 22:15-20	1 Corinthians 11:23-25
26While they were eating, Jesus took bread, said the blessing, broke it, and giving it to his disciples said, "Take and eat; this is my body."	22While they were eating, he took bread, said the blessing, broke it, and gave it to them, and said, "Take it; this is my body."	15 He said to them, "I have eagerly desired to eat this Passover with you before I suffer, 16 for, I tell you, I shall not eat it [again] until there is fulfillment in the kingdom of God." 17 Then he took a cup, gave thanks, and said, "Take this and share it among yourselves; 18 for I tell you [that] from this time on I shall not drink of the fruit of the vine until the kingdom of God comes." 19 Then he took the bread, said the blessing, broke it, and gave it to them, saying, "This is my body, which will be given for you; do this in memory of me."	23b[T]he Lord Jesus, on the night he was handed over, took bread, 24and, after he had given thanks, broke it and said, "This is my body that is for you. Do this in remembrance of me."

27Then he took a cup, gave thanks, and gave it to them,	23Then he took a cup, gave thanks, and gave it to them, and they all drank from it.	20 And likewise the cup after they had eaten,	25In the same way also the cup, after supper,
saying, "Drink from it, all of you,	24He said to them,	saying,	saying,
28for this is my blood of the covenant, which will be shed on behalf of many for the forgiveness of sins.	"This is my blood of the covenant, which will be shed for many.	"This cup is the new covenant in my blood, which will be shed for you."	"This cup is the new covenant in my blood. Do this, as often as you drink it, in remembrance of me."
29I tell you, from now on I shall not drink this fruit of the vine until the day when I drink it with you new in the kingdom of my Father."	25Amen, I say to you, I shall not drink again the fruit of the vine until the day when I drink it new in the kingdom of God."		26For as often as you eat this bread and drink the cup, you proclaim the death of the Lord until he comes.

Adapted from Jerome Kodell, *The Eucharist in the New Testament*, Zacchaeus Studies: New Testament (Collegeville, MN: Michael Glazier, 1988), 58–59.

comments to make concerning this common core and the meaning that can be taken from the probable Aramaic expressions that lie behind the Greek texts.

Ever since the Protestant Reformation, Christians have been divided about how to literally take Jesus' identification of himself with the bread and the wine of one cup, of the Last Supper. Kodell's analysis of the Last Supper texts is very informative in this matter. The phrases "This is my body" and "This is my blood" (in Mark and Matthew) are regarded as symbolic statements among many Protestants. For them, a symbol has metaphorical value, meaning the symbol calls to mind a greater reality that the symbol itself only points toward. But Kodell claims that to the mind of Palestinian Jews of the time, a "symbol" was a real thing in itself, and a symbolic event such as the words and actions of Jesus at the Last Supper brought what was symbolized into existence. Jesus, says Kodell, was saying "This is myself": he was bringing them into an intimate relationship with himself by sharing this meal with them.

Of particular importance in all four accounts is the reference to the cup as the blood of the covenant (of "the new covenant in my blood," in Paul and Luke). To Jewish thinking of the time, rooted and steeped in the Hebrew Scriptures' references to covenant and temple sacrificial practices in association with their covenant with God, there simply can be no covenant blood that was not real blood.

The Last Supper Accounts of Matthew and Mark

When comparing the four accounts it becomes apparent that Mark and Matthew have much in common, with many scholars indicating that Matthew may well have been dependent upon Mark. The reason for Matthew's willingness to borrow from Mark may be that Mark's source shows evidence, according to Kodell, of having a Palestinian origin, with the Greek showing a close relationship to an Aramaic source. As a gospel, Matthew shows the most concern for presenting Jesus from within his Jewish heritage and context. Matthew would presumably, therefore, be more than willing to draw on a Last Supper account coming from Palestine.

The Greek word employed in the Last Supper account in both Mark (14:22) and Matthew (26:26) for the phrase translated in the New American Bible as "said the blessing" is different from the Greek word translated "said the blessing" in Luke (22:19) and after he had "given thanks" (1 Cor 11:24). Mark and Matthew use *eulogesas*, which is a better Greek translation for the Hebrew word for "blessed," and Luke and Paul use *eucharistesas*, which means to give thanks (it's easy to see "Eucharist" in *eucharistesas*).

In the likelihood that Matthew borrowed from Mark in compiling his account of the Last Supper, any differences between Matthew and Mark may be considered deliberate on Matthew's part. Why would Matthew choose to make changes to Mark's account, however small? Decades of careful examination of Matthew's use of Mark have revealed that Matthew's theological perspective is different from Mark's. This doesn't mean that Matthew and Mark are ideological opponents; it simply means that Matthew wanted to emphasize certain theological insights into Jesus' life and mission while Mark had other theological insights that he wished to emphasize.

Mark was deeply concerned that his community was hesitant to embrace their call to follow Jesus if that meant suffering persecution. Mark stresses that faith in Jesus as the Messiah means acknowledging that he is the Son of God who died on a cross. Anyone who claims to be a follower of Jesus must also be willing to take up one's own cross. Mark's consistency with this message throughout his gospel is most clearly demonstrated in the many examples he gives of Jesus' disciples failing to understand the price Jesus would pay for proclaiming the good news of the kingdom of God.

Matthew has something else he wants to emphasize. While the disciples are often lacking in understanding of Jesus, Jesus never accuses them of having hardened hearts as he does in Mark (8:17; 16:14). In Matthew, Jesus' disciples are told twice that they must take up their own cross to follow him, but the path to salvation leads anyone on it to see Christ in others. It is in caring for the "least" person of note that assures one of eternal life (Matt 25:31-46).

One subtle difference between Matthew and Mark lies in their terminology for the kingdom that is at the heart of Jesus' gospel. Mark consistently refers to it as "the kingdom of God" (fourteen times). Matthew refers to the kingdom of God four or five times (early texts of Matthew 6:33 say simply, "seek first the kingdom and his righteousness"). Rather than "kingdom of God," Matthew usually refers to the "kingdom of heaven," and does so thirty-two times. Only Matthew refers to the kingdom of heaven. Luke, like Mark, refers only to the "kingdom of God" (thirty-one times). What is the difference? Matthew probably prefers calling it the kingdom of heaven because of Jewish sensitivity to keeping the name of God holy. Even in today's English, when God is capitalized it is being employed as a proper noun (i.e., a name) and not just a category of being.

Deference to the commandment to keep God's name holy (see Exod 20:7) leads Matthew to call it the kingdom of heaven, rather than the kingdom of God.

What did Jesus call it? There seems to be a preponderance of opinion that Matthew has chosen to refrain from directly quoting Jesus. But it might also be noted that if Jesus did call it the kingdom of heaven, in announcing the kingdom to Gentile audiences who were accustomed to thinking of the heavenly realm as being filled with a multitude of gods, it would make sense for Mark and Luke to emphasize the monotheistic note present in calling it the "kingdom of God."

We see something akin to this difference in Matthew 26:29 and Mark 14:25. Where Mark has Jesus saying he will not drink the fruit of the vine until he does so in the kingdom of God, Matthew has Jesus refer to the kingdom in a way that is almost completely unique: "I shall not drink this fruit of the vine until the day when I drink it with you new in the *kingdom of my Father*" (emphasis mine). Nowhere else does Jesus refer to the kingdom as the "kingdom of my Father." But note what else is different. In Mark, Jesus simply says he will not drink wine again until that future date. In Matthew, Jesus says he will not drink wine again until "I drink it with you." Earlier in Matthew (13:24-30, 36b-43), while explaining the parable of the weeds to his disciples, Jesus tells them, "Then the righteous will shine like the sun in the kingdom of their Father" (13:43). At the Last Supper, Matthew places a special emphasis on Jesus' love for his disciples in a way that stresses that Jesus and the disciples are family in the kingdom of his Father.

One important distinction between the Last Supper accounts in Matthew and Mark is to be found in the two different ways they report the same particular detail about the sharing of the cup. In Mark 14:23, we read that Jesus gave thanks for the cup, "and gave it to them, and they all drank from it." Matthew says the same thing happened, but with one key difference. Matthew tells us that Jesus, in sharing the cup with his disciples, told them, "Drink from it, all of you" (Matt 26:27). Both tell us that the disciples drank from the cup and that Jesus also said of that cup, "This is my blood of the covenant." Matthew's version, however, has a strengthened liturgical connection. Drinking from the cup is not just a historical event of the Last Supper; it is a command from Jesus that reverberates throughout history in the Eucharist.

In many other places where Matthew uses material also found in Mark, he abbreviates it. This can be seen when comparing the account of healing a leper in Mark 1:40-42 with a similar account in Matthew 8:2-3. There are thirty-nine words in Mark's account, but only twenty-eight in Matthew's. Many scholars have noted that it is actually easier to trim someone else's text for your own purposes than it is to add to it, but when someone does add to a text it is in order to emphasize certain details. In Mark 14:24 and Matthew 26:28, both Mark and Matthew report that Jesus says the blood of the covenant that this cup contains will be shed for many. Mark ends it there, but Matthew has Jesus saying more about the effect of his blood being "shed on behalf of many." It is "for the forgiveness of sins." The forgiveness of sins is certainly implicit in Mark, but Matthew makes it explicit and in doing so underlines his theology of expiation imbedded in both Jesus' death and its memorial meal, the Eucharist. Expiation is the removal of guilt or offense through an act of sacrifice.

Liturgical changes were introduced in English Masses in November 2012. One particularly contentious matter was the dropping from the eucharistic canons of the reference that the blood of Christ was shed "for all." Instead, the new canons employed Matthew and Mark's reference to "many." While it is true that "many" is a more literal translation of the Greek than "all," the change appears to some to sacrifice biblical theology for biblical literalness, at least as most people would understand the effects of the words. It now sounds like Jesus no longer died for everyone, but just for many.

Gerhard Lohfink, in his book *No Irrelevant Jesus*, includes a chapter on this very topic, and makes a significant point concerning Jesus' use of "many" instead of "all." According to Lohfink, Jesus' use of "many" was a conscious act connecting his death to that of the Suffering Servant in Isaiah 52–53. There, "many" is a reference to those outside Israel, the Gentile nations. In saying "this is my blood of the covenant, which will be shed on behalf of many for the forgiveness of sins" (Matt 26:28), he was saying that his death would bring forgiveness not only to Israel, but also to the Gentiles.

Isaiah 52:14-15

> [14]Even as many were amazed at him—
>> so marred were his features,
>> beyond that of mortals
>> his appearance, beyond that of human beings—
> [15]So shall he startle many nations,
>> kings shall stand speechless;
> For those who have not been told shall see,
>> those who have not heard shall ponder it.

Isaiah 53:11-12

> [11]Because of his anguish he shall see the light;
>> because of his knowledge he shall be content;
> My servant, the just one, shall justify the many,
>> their iniquity he shall bear.
> [12]Therefore I will give him his portion among the many,
>> and he shall divide the spoils with the mighty,
> Because he surrendered himself to death,
>> was counted among the transgressors,
> Bore the sins of many,
>> and interceded for the transgressors.

The Last Supper Accounts in Luke and Paul

Paul's account of the Last Supper is the earliest account, and yet it has several features that show the greatest similarities to Luke's account. While scholars generally do not believe Paul was the source for Luke's account, the fact that they bear so much similarity to each other is an indication of how faithfully Last Supper accounts were handed on over time.

Speeches are very important to Luke and we find many of them in Luke and Acts. The gospel begins with eloquent orations from Zechariah and Mary. During his ministry, Jesus delivers the sermon on the plain (Luke 6:20-49) as well as many parables, some of the best known of which are unique to Luke. In Acts, both Peter and Paul evangelize with powerful speeches. Luke's account of the Last Supper is longer than Matthew's, Mark's, or Paul's, and part of the reason it is lengthier is because Luke's account can be read as Jesus' farewell discourse, a type of speech with a long literary tradition.

Farewell discourses typically arise when leaders who are aware of their impending departure or death bid farewell by issuing final instructions and expressing their concern for the future well-being of the company they have led (as in Jacob's farewell in Genesis 48–50). These matters are certainly evident in Jesus' address to his apostles at the Last Supper (Luke 22:14-34).

In verse 15 he warns them of what lies ahead of him and in verses 17-18 he offers them the bread and wine that are then and henceforth to be his sustaining presence in their midst (this becomes abundantly clear in the meals he shares with them after the resurrection). After warning them that he is about to be betrayed by one of their own numbers, their response to this news is to "debate among themselves who among them would do such a deed" (v. 23). But this debate quickly turns to claims of their own greatness (v. 24). Just as Peter will claim that he is prepared to suffer much for Jesus' sake (v. 33), they all evidently claim that their boundless loyalty to Jesus would make betrayal impossible.

Jesus responds to their claims of greatness by granting them a final instruction concerning how they must henceforth relate to each other. They aren't to be like worldly leaders; they are to be like Jesus, serving each other in humility (vv. 25-27). After teaching them the need for humility, and knowing that they will all abandon him shortly, he nevertheless assures them of their greatness because of their loyalty: "It is you who have stood by me in my trials; and I confer a kingdom on you, just as my Father has conferred one on me, that you may eat and drink at my table in my kingdom; and you will sit on thrones judging the twelve tribes of Israel" (vv. 28-30).

There will be no need to vie with each other for greatness; he has assured all of them of their greatness.

That Luke's expanded emphasis on Jesus' concern for the well-being of his apostles occurs at the Last Supper is in keeping with Luke's portrayal of Jesus' entire ministry being centered on fellowship around a table. As a prophetic encounter with his death, the Last Supper in Luke is portrayed as the culmination of Jesus' commitment to his followers and to all whom in the future would share a meal with him in the Eucharist. The Lukan theme of Eucharist as fellowship with Jesus is subtly present early on in his account. It can be detected in his instructions to Peter and John to obtain a place to eat the Passover meal: "When the day of the feast of Unleavened Bread arrived, the day for sacrificing the Passover lamb, he sent out Peter and John, instructing them, 'Go and make preparations for us to eat the Passover' " (22:7-8).

In Luke, the Passover meal is a communal celebration of the "us" that is Jesus and his apostles. That is an emphasis missing in Mark. In Mark, it is the disciples who approach Jesus concerning his celebration of the Passover: "On the first day of the Feast of Unleavened Bread, when they sacrificed the Passover lamb, his disciples said to him, 'Where do you want us to go and prepare for you to eat the Passover?' " (14:12).

This pervasive Lukan theme of table fellowship continues at the Passover as Jesus instructs Peter and John as to how they are to make their inquiries: "When you go into the city, a man will meet you carrying a jar of water. Follow him into the house that he enters and say to the master of the house, 'The teacher says to you, "Where is the guest room where I may eat the Passover with my disciples?" ' " (Luke 22:10-11).

When they arrive at the place and all is made ready, Jesus explicitly states his deeply felt importance of sharing this meal with his disciples, even though, as we learn later (22:21, 31), Jesus knows his betrayer is among them and that they will all abandon him: "When the hour came, he took his place at table with the apostles. He said to them, 'I have eagerly desired to eat this Passover with you before I suffer, for, I tell you, I shall not eat it [again] until there is fulfillment in the kingdom of God'" (22:14-16).

Luke's expanded account of the Last Supper is the only account to mention a second cup, but that is a detail that helps us recognize that he is authentically describing a Jewish festive meal, one that Luke understands to be the Passover (see Luke 22:7, 15). By comparison to Mark and Matthew, however, Luke presents two theologically important changes to the order of events.

The first switch in the order of things comes as soon as Jesus takes his place at the table, right after he tells the apostles of his great desire to eat the Passover with them. This is when, in Luke, Jesus tells his apostles, "I tell you, I shall not eat it [again] until there is fulfillment in the kingdom of God" (22:16), and "from this time on I shall not drink of the fruit of the vine until the kingdom of God comes" (22:18). In Matthew (26:29) and Mark (14:25), Jesus tells the apostles that he will not drink wine again until he drinks it "new" in the kingdom of heaven (of God, in Mark). He does not mention eating.

This is an eschatological feature of the Last Supper (that is, it concerns the ultimate fulfillment of God's plan of salvation) that appears in part in all three Synoptic Gospels. By placing it prior to the sharing of the bread and cup during the Last Supper, Luke is emphasizing the eschatological nature of the Eucharist. We will investigate this more thoroughly when we look at the meals Jesus partook with his disciples in Luke after the resurrection.

Second, Jesus does not announce that his betrayer is in their midst until after the sharing of the bread that is his body and the cup that is the new covenant in his blood. That his betrayer (Judas Iscariot) is among those who have shared his body and blood is a Lukan concern for the health of the Christian communities who will share Eucharist together after the resurrection. This concern arises in the account of the attempted deception of Ananias and Sapphira in Acts 5:1-11.

Comparing Luke's (and Paul's) account of the Last Supper with Matthew's and Mark's yields another important nuance conveyed by a single word. In both Matthew and Mark, Jesus tells the disciples that the cup they share is the "blood of the covenant." In Luke (and in 1 Corinthians) Jesus tells them, "This cup is the *new* covenant in my blood" (22:20, emphasis mine). In Matthew and Mark the covenant in Jesus' blood need not be distinguished from the original covenant God made with his people through Moses. The covenant God made with his people through Moses was sanctified and ratified by the blood of an animal (Exod 24:5-8). In Matthew and Mark God's covenant with his people is sealed by Jesus' own blood, the blood of the Son of God. This makes the covenant unshakeable and far more profound, but it is only in the Last Supper discourses of Luke and Paul that the realization emerges that the profundity of the covenant in Jesus' blood is so great that it is an altogether new covenant between God and mankind.

The theology behind the accounts in Matthew and Mark, however, remains true even though the covenant ratified in Jesus' blood is also a new covenant. The new covenant does not replace the old one because it is also a covenant made out of God's fidelity to the earlier one.

Sharing a Meal with the Risen Christ

Luke 24:13-35

[13]Now that very day two of them were going to a village seven miles from Jerusalem called Emmaus, [14]and they were conversing about all the things that had occurred. [15]And it happened that while they were conversing and debating, Jesus himself drew near and walked with them, [16]but their eyes were prevented from recognizing him. [17]He asked them, "What are you discussing as you walk along?" They stopped, looking downcast. [18]One of them, named Cleopas, said to him in reply, "Are you the only visitor to Jerusalem who does not know of the things that have taken place there in these days?" [19]And he replied to them, "What sort of things?" They said to him, "The things that happened to Jesus the Nazarene, who was a prophet mighty in deed and word before God and all the people, [20]how our chief priests and rulers both handed him over to a sentence of death and crucified him. [21]But we were hoping that he would be the one to redeem Israel; and besides all this, it is now the third day since this took place. [22]Some women from our group, however, have astounded us: they were at the tomb early in the morning [23]and did not find his body; they came back and reported that they had indeed seen a vision of angels who announced that he was alive. [24]Then some of those with us went to the tomb and found things just as the women had described, but him they did not see." [25]And he said to them, "Oh, how foolish you are! How slow of heart to believe all that the prophets

spoke! [26]Was it not necessary that the Messiah should suffer these things and enter into his glory?" [27]Then beginning with Moses and all the prophets, he interpreted to them what referred to him in all the scriptures. [28]As they approached the village to which they were going, he gave the impression that he was going on farther. [29]But they urged him, "Stay with us, for it is nearly evening and the day is almost over." So he went in to stay with them. [30]And it happened that, while he was with them at table, he took bread, said the blessing, broke it, and gave it to them. [31]With that their eyes were opened and they recognized him, but he vanished from their sight. [32]Then they said to each other, "Were not our hearts burning [within us] while he spoke to us on the way and opened the scriptures to us?" [33]So they set out at once and returned to Jerusalem where they found gathered together the eleven and those with them [34]who were saying, "The Lord has truly been raised and has appeared to Simon!" [35]Then the two recounted what had taken place on the way and how he was made known to them in the breaking of the bread.

Only Luke gives us this account of the two erstwhile disciples of Jesus who encounter him as the risen one while dolefully making their way to a village called Emmaus. They are not simply mourning the loss of Jesus; they are mourning the loss of their own hopes and their own vision of what it would have meant if Jesus had been the Messiah they sought after.

In their grief they have abandoned both faith and hope. It is perhaps an act of generosity that Luke calls them disciples at this point, because without Jesus' personal encounter with them they might never again have considered themselves followers of a mistaken messiah, one whose death by crucifixion brought shame not just to his followers, but was a way for the Roman occupiers to mock the entire nation.

All the while Jesus instructs them about the necessity of the Messiah suffering and how the Scriptures testify to that necessity, they still do not recognize him, but they are fascinated enough about their new companion's teaching that they offer him the hospitality of food and shelter when they arrive at their destination. What happens next goes against the rules of hospitality, however, for it is their guest who takes the bread, says the blessing, and breaks it in order to serve his hosts.

As an account of a resurrection appearance, the appearance on the road to Emmaus is unique because its emphasis is actually on how Christians to whom there have been no resurrection appearance are to recognize the risen Christ in their midst. There are many hidden gems in this account, but a special one that has been unearthed by Francis Moloney, SDB, in *A Body Broken for a Broken People*, is very poignant in relation to the Eucharist. Having risen from the dead, Jesus sets about immediately to heal his disciples and to strengthen them for spreading the Gospel to the ends of the earth. The healing for these broken, discouraged disciples comes from the risen Christ, but in the context of the Eucharist, a Eucharist that includes the breaking open of Scripture and the breaking of the bread.

In the moment they recognize him, Jesus disappears from their sight, but not from their lives. They are empowered now to be disciples and they immediately return to Jerusalem because the mission of the disciples to "be my witnesses . . . to the ends of the earth" (Acts 1:8) is to begin in Jerusalem. The risen Lord will appear off and on for forty days (Acts 1:3) and much later to Paul, but other than that, the risen Lord is to be known throughout time, until his coming again, in the breaking of the bread. It is in the Eucharist that we recognize the risen Lord.

CHAPTER FOUR

The Eucharist in Paul and Acts

In this chapter, we want to look at how the New Testament either describes or hints at the celebration of Eucharist among Christians in the first century following the resurrection. Because the Gospel of John was the last gospel to be written, John's theology of the Eucharist reveals its greatest rewards when we bring to it an appreciation for what Eucharist meant for Christians earlier in the first century.

Breaking Bread Together

According to Luke in the Acts of the Apostles, the early faithful responders to the apostles' message concerning Jesus' life, death, and resurrection were called followers of "the Way" (six times in Acts—18:25, 26; 19:9, 23; 24:14, 22) and/or Nazoreans (24:5) as well as (and perhaps before) Christians (11:26). It would also take some time before Christians in a specific community would be understood as constituting a "church." Of all the gospels, only Matthew uses the term "church" as something Jesus actually named in reference to his mission (16:18; 18:17). Acts describes the first community of believers as faithful Jews who met together in the Jewish temple area on a daily basis while also living a vigorous communal life together as followers of Jesus and adherents of the apostles' teachings.

Their own understanding of who they were didn't develop as quickly as their appreciation of *whose* they were, but the former gradually grew out of the latter. Nevertheless, from the very beginning, there was one constancy to a gathering of Jesus followers: they broke bread together.

Acts 2:38-47

> [38]Peter [said] to them, "Repent and be baptized, every one of you, in the name of Jesus Christ for the forgiveness of your sins; and you will receive the gift of the holy Spirit. [39]For the promise is made to you and to your children and to all those far off, whomever the Lord our God will call." [40]He testified with many other arguments, and was exhorting them, "Save yourselves from this corrupt generation." [41]Those who accepted his message were baptized, and about three thousand persons were added that day.
>
> **Communal Life.** [42]They devoted themselves to the teaching of the apostles and to the communal life, to the breaking of the bread and to the prayers. [43]Awe came upon everyone, and many wonders and signs were done through the apostles. [44]All who believed were together and had all things in common; [45]they would sell their property and possessions and divide them among all according to each one's need. [46]Every day they devoted themselves to meeting together in the temple area and to breaking bread in their homes. They ate their meals with exultation and sincerity of heart, [47]praising God and enjoying favor with all the people. And every day the Lord added to their number those who were being saved.

The book of Acts describes the early and rapid growth of those who accepted Jesus as the Messiah due to the preaching of Peter and the other apostles. In the instance above, three thousand were added to the movement in a single day. This community of early believers was extremely tight-knit. On the practical level, they pooled all their property and resources so that there was no one among them lacking in any essential. As believers, they grew in their faith by their attentiveness to the teaching of the apostles, "to the breaking of the bread," and their devotion in prayer. As found in verse 42, the breaking of the bread is usually understood as the celebration of Eucharist, but there are two different contexts in Acts 2:42-47 for "breaking bread." In Acts 2:42 the definite article is used (*the* breaking of *the* bread), and this bread breaking occurs in the context of the entire community of believers gathering together. In Acts 2:46 the "breaking bread" occurs "in their homes," followed by a notice: "They ate their meals with exultation and sincerity of heart."

What this probably is telling us is that when gathering together with the apostles, the breaking of the bread was done as Jesus commanded, "in memory of me" (Luke 22:19), and was truly a celebration of Eucharist. But outside of those times, when Christians ate together in their homes, there was a strong communal memory, inculcated by the teaching of the apostles, of those many meals to which Jesus invited sinners to join him in anticipation of the great messianic wedding feast. Whenever new followers gathered together to eat, they would also break bread together, and they did so knowing that Jesus was present to them: "For where two or three are gathered together in my name, there am I in the midst of them" (Matt 18:20). While these latter meals were not the Eucharist, they were meals where the love of Christ in their midst was strongly felt and was a cause for rejoicing. Hopefully, gatherings at mealtime between Christian families and/or guests, whether in private homes or at church potlucks or picnics, are still occasions for welcoming the presence of Christ into fellowship with those who call upon his name.

The Religious Connotations of Eating

Many Catholics remember the time before Vatican II when every Friday of the year was a day of abstinence, a day when we abstained from eating any meat except for fish. While we continue the practice of abstinence during Fridays of Lent, there are national conferences of bishops around the globe that have sought to reinstate abstinence from meat on all Fridays. As it is, though, the consideration of food as part of one's religious observance is not prevalent in the Western world. Jews who observe kosher food laws and Muslims who eat according to Halal regulations are far more aware of the importance of food to their religious practice than most Christians, Seventh Day Adventists being a notable exception.

In the early days of Christianity awareness of the food one ate was of great religious importance, however. The first mention of food creating a problem between Christians appears in Acts 6:1-7 when the Greek speaking Jewish Christians complained to the apostles that their widows were not being given the same food rations as the Hebrew (Aramaic) speaking widows. The need to address this matter led the apostles to appoint deacons to oversee the just distribution of food to all widows. The importance of this to a religious awareness of food ought to be obvious. Food is essential to life and the faithful must consider the just distribution of food a matter of conscience.

It was not long before a major issue arose among Christians concerning what food could be eaten. This arose when the Gospel began to attract numbers of Gentiles to the faith. Until then, there was no question over whether followers of the Messiah would practice traditional Jewish food rules, such as avoiding pork or any meat from animals that did not have a cloven hoof and chew the cud (see Lev 11:1-47).

Once Gentiles were baptized in large numbers, there began a period of great tension and dispute that took many years, if not decades, to resolve. The utter lack of dietary regulations among Gentile converts was an exceptionally serious problem whenever and wherever they gathered for Christian fellowship with Jewish Christians, because Christians first gathered together in private homes and the pinnacle of worship for both was the Eucharist, which occurred in the context of a meal, the agape feast.

Practicing Jews were not even supposed to enter Gentile homes or eat with Gentiles because of the many ways in which Gentiles violated the rules of religious purity (including the touching of animal and human corpses). Entering a Gentile home or eating with a Gentile would render a practicing Jew unclean and therefore unfit for temple worship or association with other Jews in their own household.

The Baptism of a Gentile

The first extensive account of a Gentile's baptism is described in Acts and highlights the religious hurdles that had to be overcome. Just as the coming of the Messiah into the world had to be made known through revelation by an angel, the first entry of a Gentile into the messianic fold required direct revelation. The Gentile was a Roman centurion, who was also "devout and God-fearing along with his whole household, who used to give alms generously to the Jewish people and pray to God constantly" (Acts 10:2). Acts 10:1–11:18 is a lengthy, detailed account of how Peter became convinced through a vision that it was God's will for him to enter Cornelius's house in Caesarea and to baptize him and his entire household.

For brevity's sake it will be retold here in summary fashion. First, Cornelius himself receives an angelic vision telling him that God has accepted his prayers and almsgiving and that as a reward he should send messengers to summon a certain Simon called Peter. Before they arrive where Peter is staying (at a house in Joppa), Peter has a rather bizarre vision of all sorts of beasts Jews are forbidden to eat being set before him with the command to "slaughter and eat." Peter balks, saying he has never touched unclean food, but the voice of the vision warns, "What God has made clean, you are not to call profane" (10:15). Peter still needs convincing, and so the vision and the message are presented to him three times. The messengers from Cornelius arrive and bring Peter to the Gentile's house, which is now filled with all Cornelius's friends and relatives.

Standing outside his house, Cornelius meets Peter, who immediately explains to Cornelius how he came to even broach the idea of meeting with him: "You know that it is unlawful for a Jewish man to associate with, or visit, a Gentile, but God has shown me that I should not call any person profane or unclean. And that is why I came without objection when sent for" (10:28-29).

Once inside Cornelius's house, Peter proclaims the Gospel of salvation in Jesus Christ, who was sent to the Israelites, but "who is Lord of all" (10:36). Cornelius and his entire household listen to the Good News and believe, and upon believing, are filled with the Holy Spirit. God has now brought Peter, the Jewish apostle of a Jewish Messiah, through two visions and an outpouring of the Holy Spirit, to the point where he can now fully acknowledge that Gentiles too will become part of "the Way." Even those Jews accompanying Peter have to give up their prejudices: "The circumcised believers who had accompanied Peter were astounded that the gift of the holy Spirit should have been poured out on the Gentiles also, for they could hear them speaking in tongues and glorifying God. Then Peter responded, 'Can anyone withhold the water for baptizing these people, who have received the holy Spirit even as we have?' He ordered them to be baptized in the name of Jesus Christ. Then they invited him to stay for a few days" (10:45-49).

When Peter eventually returns to Jerusalem, what he has done has already been reported to his fellow Jewish believers, and they accuse him of violating the faith: "Now the apostles and the brothers who were in Judea heard that the Gentiles too had accepted the word of God. So when Peter went up to Jerusalem the circumcised believers confronted him, saying, 'You entered the house of uncircumcised people and ate with them'" (11:1-3).

Are his fellow apostles among those believers who confront him? It might take some reading between the lines, but as we will see shortly, apostles did get into arguments with each other. What we do read plainly, however, is that Peter explained himself and his willingness to baptize Cornelius by way of the visions and the irresistible evidence of the Holy Spirit's presence in Cornelius and his household. "When they heard this," we are told in Acts 11:18, "they stopped objecting and glorified God, saying, 'God has then granted life-giving repentance to the Gentiles too.'"

The Eucharist and Fellowship with Gentiles

The inclusion of Gentiles to the faith spreads as Greek speaking Jewish believers begin to proclaim the Gospel to non-Jews in Antioch, and the numbers of Gentile believers grow to such a size that these believers are given a new name: Christians.

Acts 11:19-26

> [19]Now those who had been scattered by the persecution that arose because of Stephen went as far as Phoenicia, Cyprus, and Antioch, preaching the word to no one but Jews. [20]There were some Cypriots and Cyrenians among them, however, who came to Antioch and began to speak to the Greeks as well, proclaiming the Lord Jesus. [21]The hand of the Lord was with them and a great number who believed turned to the Lord. [22]The news about them reached the ears of the church in Jerusalem, and they sent Barnabas [to go] to Antioch. [23]When he arrived and saw the grace of God, he rejoiced and encouraged them all to remain faithful to the Lord in firmness of heart, [24]for he was a good man, filled with the holy Spirit and faith. And a large number of people was added to the Lord. [25]Then he went to Tarsus to look for Saul, [26]and when he had found him he brought him to Antioch. For a whole year they met with the church and taught a large number of people, and it was in Antioch that the disciples were first called Christians.

The number of converts in Antioch was so large that both Peter and Paul, the once rabid persecutor of those who dared call Jesus "Messiah," are actively ministering to the faithful there, and presumably heading up some of the evangelization efforts. In Acts, Luke downplays the mounting controversy among Jesus' Jewish followers over the importance of Jewish religious practices, not least of which was circumcision as the essential sign to Jewish males of their covenantal relationship with God. What about these new Gentile Christians? Ought they be circumcised? There is a noticeable silence in Acts as to whether after being baptized Cornelius also accepted circumcision. Lest we think Peter was immediately of the mind that circumcision should not be imposed on Gentile converts, attention must be paid to a heated exchange Paul had with Peter in Antioch over relationships between Jewish and Gentile Christians.

Paul never minced his words, not just when championing the cause of accepting Gentiles into the faith without circumcision, but also in warning Gentile converts that becoming circumcised was hazardous to their relationship with Christ. If they became circumcised, they would become cursed, condemned to fulfilling every iota of the Mosaic Law without recourse to Jesus' free gift of salvation (Gal 3:1-10).

In Acts, chapters 10–11, Luke moves from Peter baptizing the Gentile Cornelius to the evangelization of Gentiles in Antioch and concludes with Saul and Barnabas being placed in charge of fundraising among Gentiles for famine relief among Jewish Christians in Judah. In this way, Luke presents the mutual love of Christians of diverse backgrounds. While he does tell us of Jewish opposition to the Good News in Acts 14:1-7, we only hear about the controversy between Jewish Christians and Paul in the account of the Council of Jerusalem. Here, in Acts 15:1-35, Luke presents the apostles and James of Jerusalem unanimously rejecting the need to circumcise Gentiles who have come to faith. The cause of the controversy only occupies a single sentence, in Acts 15:1: "Some who had come down from Judea were instructing the brothers, 'Unless you are circumcised according to the Mosaic practice, you cannot be saved.'"

Luke emphasizes that the apostolic efforts to spread the Good News of Jesus Christ as Lord of all—from Jerusalem, through all of Judea and Samaria and to the ends of the earth— was successful. And it was! But it was not part of Luke's agenda to describe in detail the internal turmoil among Jesus' followers as they struggled on the road to success. While writing the Galatians to remind them that their faith in Jesus was the source of their salvation and that circumcision had nothing to offer them but trouble, Paul told them of a rift that occurred between him and Peter. It was a rift over Peter aligning himself with Jewish Christians by refusing to eat with Gentile Christians.

Galatians 2:11-14

> [11]And when Cephas came to Antioch, I opposed him to his face because he clearly was wrong. [12]For, until some people came from James, he used to eat with the Gentiles; but when they came, he began to draw back and separated himself, because he was afraid of the circumcised. [13]And the rest of the Jews [also] acted hypocritically along with him, with the result that even Barnabas was carried away by their hypocrisy. [14]But when I saw that they were not on the right road in line with the truth of the gospel, I said to Cephas in front of all, "If you, though a Jew, are living like a Gentile and not like a Jew, how can you compel the Gentiles to live like Jews?"

There is little doubt among scholars that by refusing to eat with Gentile Christians, Peter was also refusing to share Eucharist with them, as Eucharist took place in the context of the agape meal. Scholars are divided over whether Paul's confrontation with Peter over his hypocrisy occurred before or after the Jerusalem council's historic decision to reject the need to circumcise Gentile converts. Whether it was before or after, it shows that while Peter could accept the faith of Gentiles, he was uneasy being thought of as "unclean" by associating with them. Then, as now, the greatest sign of Christian unity lies in the sharing of Eucharist. Perhaps a significant signpost on the road back to communion with those whom we cannot share Eucharist might be our coming together to share meals in Christian fraternity, with a keen awareness that whenever we share a meal together in Jesus' name, he will be in our midst (Matt 18:20).

The Problems Associated with Eating Meat

What and where Gentiles ate was a problem that Paul had to struggle with in ways that went beyond questions of circumcision and Jewish food regulations. In First Corinthians Paul has to confront a food controversy that divides Gentile Christians from other Gentile Christians. In the cities of the Roman Empire there were always one or more temples dedicated to particular deities of either the Roman Pantheon or those worshiped by subject people. A vital part of temple worship (as also in the Jewish temple in Jerusalem) was animal sacrifice. The gods of the empire were so popular that it was difficult to find meat available for sale that had not been sacrificed in an act of worship at one of the temples first.

What were new converts to Christ to do if they had an appetite for meat? Paul had no problem with them eating pork, but what if the pork had been sacrificed to Zeus before being sold in the local meat markets, which were often attached to a temple?

Paul deals with this matter in his Letter to the Romans (14:1–15:6). There, he discusses it in terms of Christians' conscience. If Christians are "strong" and know that these other so-called gods are not gods, then they do not sin in eating food that has been sacrificed to idols—unless, their eating it scandalizes those who are weak in conscience who might follow their example only to have their conscience condemn them. For Paul, what you eat is not a private concern; what you eat is always a means to nourish good harmony in the local church.

He takes a different approach to the problem in First Corinthians. Interestingly, Paul wrote Romans while in Corinth, and perhaps only a year or less after writing First Corinthians. The biggest difference between the two approaches is that in First Corinthians he situates the problem of eating food sacrificed to idols by contrasting idol worship with the Eucharist. Apparently, in writing the Romans, whom he had never visited, he dealt with the problem in terms of simply having food available to eat that had once been sacrificed in a temple. There is no indication that the Roman Christians were even seeking his advice on the matter. In writing the Romans Paul wanted to present his teachings in a way that would win their favor, so that when he did visit them, they would not only receive him warmly, but help finance a planned voyage to Spain (Rom 15:24, 28-29). But in writing the Corinthians, he was addressing a church he personally founded and which was seeking his help in dealing with issues that were disturbing the peace of the community.

In the process of addressing the issue of eating food sacrificed to idols, Paul makes one of the clearest statements in the New Testament concerning our communion with Christ in the Eucharist and our subsequent communion with one another.

1 Corinthians 10:16-31

[16]The cup of blessing that we bless, is it not a participation in the blood of Christ? The bread that we break, is it not a participation in the body of Christ? [17]Because the loaf of bread is one, we, though many, are one body, for we all partake of the one loaf.

[18]Look at Israel according to the flesh; are not those who eat the sacrifices participants in the altar? [19]So what am I saying? That meat sacrificed to idols is anything? Or that an idol is anything? [20]No, I mean that what they sacrifice, [they sacrifice] to demons, not to God, and I do not want you to become participants with demons. [21]You cannot drink the cup of the Lord and also the cup of demons. You cannot partake of the table of the Lord and of the table of demons. [22]Or are we provoking the Lord to jealous anger? Are we stronger than he?

Seek the Good of Others. [23]"Everything is lawful," but not everything is beneficial. "Everything is lawful," but not everything builds up. [24]No one should seek his own advantage, but that of his neighbor. [25]Eat anything sold in the market, without raising questions on grounds of conscience, [26]for "the earth and its fullness are the Lord's." [27]If an unbeliever invites you and you want to go, eat whatever is placed before you, without raising questions on grounds of conscience. [28]But if someone says to you, "This was offered in sacrifice," do not eat it on account of the one who called attention to it and on account of conscience; [29]I mean not your own conscience, but the other's. For why should my freedom be determined by someone else's conscience? [30]If I partake thankfully, why am I reviled for that over which I give thanks?

[31]So whether you eat or drink, or whatever you do, do everything for the glory of God.

Notice the double use of "bless" in verse 16: "The cup of *bless*ing that we *bless*" [emphasis added]. It's easy to let our eyes slide over that while our minds focus on the cup, which is singular. We know Paul is talking about the cup that is the cup of our Lord's blood given to us in Eucharist, but, as Raymond F. Collins notes in his *Sacra Pagina* commentary on First Corinthians, Paul is not describing two different rituals concerning the cup, rather he is describing the result of liturgical prayer. In eucharistic liturgy the cup is blessed and it becomes for us God's blessing to us. God's blessing to us is to bring us into participation in the blood of Christ.

The word translated here as "participation" is a very rich word in New Testament usage, and it gets translated in a variety of ways. The Greek word is *koinonia*. It is also translated as "fellowship." That is how Paul uses it in his thanksgiving for the Corinthians just after he greets them in the opening of this letter: "God is faithful, and by him you were called to fellowship with his Son, Jesus Christ our Lord" (1 Cor 1:9).

It is worth reading all of this thanksgiving, from verse 4 through verse 9, because it actually describes the spiritual riches God bestows on the Corinthians, all of which arise from their *koinonia* with Christ, and the cup of blessing is that same *koinonia* that they have in the blood of Christ.

1 Corinthians 1:4-9

> [4]I give thanks to my God always on your account for the grace of God bestowed on you in Christ Jesus, [5]that in him you were enriched in every way, with all discourse and all knowledge, [6]as the testimony to Christ was confirmed among you, [7]so that you are not lacking in any spiritual gift as you wait for the revelation of our Lord Jesus Christ. [8]He will keep you firm to the end, irreproachable on the day of our Lord Jesus [Christ]. [9]God is faithful, and by him you were called to fellowship with his Son, Jesus Christ our Lord.

That they have gained fellowship in Christ means that God has enriched them with every spiritual gift, including "discourse and all knowledge." This discourse and knowledge would include the spiritual words of nourishment from Scripture, the proclamation of the gospel and inspired preaching, along with the subsequent understanding of what God has done and will do for them in Christ. In having these gifts, God will keep them safely his until their salvation is fully revealed "on the day of our Lord Jesus [Christ]." All of this is in and through their calling by God into "fellowship" (*koinonia*) with Jesus Christ. Paul recalls that *koinonia* by reference to its actuality in the cup and bread that are the body and blood of Christ in order to warn them against having *koinonia* with demons by drinking and eating in the sacrificial rites of pagan temples (1 Cor 10:16-31).

The Eucharist and the Agape Meal

Paul's dealings with the Corinthians provides us with the clearest picture we have in the New Testament concerning the celebration of Eucharist in the early church—but to be precise, it should be specified that it describes the attempted celebration of Eucharist within a Pauline church. The *Didache*, which is a noncanonical text dating perhaps as early as some New Testament texts, provides some variations in eucharistic celebrations, but these were not normative. Indeed, Paul and the Last Supper accounts of the Synoptic Gospels record what are believed to be liturgical traditions of prayers of institution used by early churches during Eucharist. The words of institution found in Paul and the Synoptics have clearly lent themselves to the eucharistic liturgies of Catholic, Orthodox, and many Protestant communions.

In *St. Paul's Corinth* the late Pauline scholar Jerome Murphy-O'Connor delved deep into history, archaeology, geography, and, of course, Paul's letters to the Corinthians in order to provide us the fullest picture possible of these early Christians in Corinth, Greece, and their attempts to celebrate Eucharist.

Corinth was not a frontier city, but it had its similarities. At the time of First Corinthians, it was a city less than a hundred years old, built to serve the needs of the Roman Empire to handle the busy trade between two major parts of Greece and to serve as a shipping corridor between the Aegean and Ionian Seas. The Romans had destroyed the original Corinth in 146 BC, but Julius Caesar rebuilt it in 44 BC and it had to be repopulated to serve the empire's interests. As the economic and political center of Greece, its official language was Latin. Unlike more established cities in the Roman Empire, Corinth was seen as a city of promise to the large class of noncitizens made up of former slaves, known as freedmen. In Corinth, freed slaves and their children could hope to enter fairly lucrative businesses in the new and bustling trade market, and they could also aspire to some level of prominence in both the government and the social hierarchy of the community.

When Paul tells the Corinthians to look at themselves and to recognize that "[n]ot many of you were wise by human standards, not many were powerful, not many were of noble birth" (1 Cor 1:26), he does not say that none of them were, and, in Corinth, it certainly didn't mean they lacked people with aspiration. If they weren't born into nobility, they could still hope to buy themselves into some semblance of significance. There appears to have been a wealthy minority in Corinth that even turned the Eucharist into an opportunity to show how much better they enjoyed life than their poorer brothers and sisters in Christ.

The church in Corinth was a house church (1 Cor 16:19; see also Rom 16:5; Col 4:15; Phlm 1:2), an association of Christians who met in a single home for their eucharistic gatherings. At least one surprising aspect of the Corinthian church may be how small a community had to be in order to gather in a private home. Murphy-O'Connor tells us that archaeological findings in Corinth itself make it almost certain that Paul is addressing a community of no more than fifty people at the very most. In all likelihood it was even smaller. Forty seems to be a safer guess. Between those named in Acts and in Paul's letters as being members of the church in Corinth, Murphy-O'Connor counts a total of thirty as having been identified by name in the New Testament. There are those who believe that Paul must have been addressing more than one house church in his letters to the Corinthians, which might greatly expand the number of Christians in Corinth, but there is no internal evidence in his letters to indicate this.

The average area of dining rooms from six houses excavated from the time was less than four hundred square feet, but by Roman custom these dining rooms (*triclinium* in Latin) contained couches around a wall where diners would recline, making the typical maximum number of diners in the dining room to be limited to only nine. This means that most of the Christians attending an agape meal at a house church in Corinth could not have met in the dining room. The most logical space for the remainder would have been the atrium, where they would have been seated on the stone floor rather than reclining on couches.

Paul tells the Corinthians that the tradition behind their eucharistic liturgies is one that comes from the Lord himself, during the Last Supper. It is also unmistakable that their celebrations of Eucharist are taking place during a full meal (at least for some), in one of what the Letter of Jude calls love (*agape*) feasts (v. 12). The agape meals did not simply disappear all at once. In some places it took two or three centuries. But wherever and whenever the agape meals disappeared, the Eucharist then became an occasion where only consecrated bread and wine were served to the faithful. Even after the Eucharist was separated from a fuller meal, Christians continued to feast together as a local church-sanctioned, religious activity. Perhaps today church potlucks and picnics might count as more modern versions of the agape meal.

Such a possibility seems not only to have existed, but perhaps was actually quite common throughout churches of the time. At Corinth, at the time of Paul's first letter, a specific breaking of bread and a specific cup of wine were given during the context of a fuller meal as the body and blood of the Lord, just as during the Last Supper. Paul does not fault the Corinthians for celebrating Eucharist during an agape meal. It is, however, the way that the fuller meal fails the test of Christian fellowship that brings Paul's rebuke.

The way the Corinthians are conducting their agape meals is so scandalous that it leads Paul to reject the idea that they are actually also celebrating Eucharist. It may well be that the abuses Paul condemned in Corinth were similar to problems experienced in many other locations, and that these problems help explain why the agape meal was disassociated from the Eucharist.

1 Corinthians 11:17-34

An Abuse at Corinth. [17]In giving this instruction, I do not praise the fact that your meetings are doing more harm than good. [18]First of all, I hear that when you meet as a church there are divisions among you, and to a degree I believe it; [19]there have to be factions among you in order that [also] those who are approved among you may become known. [20]When you meet in one place, then, it is not to eat the Lord's supper, [21]for in eating, each one goes ahead with his own supper, and one goes hungry while another gets drunk. [22]Do you not have houses in which you can eat and drink? Or do you show contempt for the church of God and make those who have nothing feel ashamed? What can I say to you? Shall I praise you? In this matter I do not praise you.

Tradition of the Institution. [23]For I received from the Lord what I also handed on to you, that the Lord Jesus, on the night he was handed over, took bread, [24]and, after he had given thanks, broke it and said, "This is my body that is for you. Do this in remembrance of me." [25]In the same way also the cup, after supper, saying, "This cup is the new covenant in my blood. Do this, as often as you drink it, in remembrance of me." [26]For as often as you eat this bread and drink the cup, you proclaim the death of the Lord until he comes.

[27]Therefore whoever eats the bread or drinks the cup of the Lord unworthily will have to answer for the body and blood of the Lord. [28]A person should examine himself, and so eat the bread and drink the cup. [29]For anyone who eats and drinks without discerning the body, eats and drinks judgment on himself. [30]That is why many among you are ill and infirm, and a considerable number are dying.

[31]If we discerned ourselves, we would not be under judgment; [32]but since we are judged by [the] Lord, we are being disciplined so that we may not be condemned along with the world.

[33]Therefore, my brothers, when you come together to eat, wait for one another. [34]If anyone is hungry, he should eat at home, so that your meetings may not result in judgment. The other matters I shall set in order when I come.

What appears to have been happening in Corinth is that the agape meal was being celebrated in an unequitable fashion. The agape and Eucharist would take place on Sunday, "the Lord's Day," as it became known among early Christians in recognition of the resurrection occurring on Sunday (see Acts 20:7; 1 Cor 16:2; Rev 1:9-11).

Guests of honor would be received in the dining room (the *triclinium*), where they would recline on comfortable couches and be treated to a sumptuous meal, probably provided by the wealthy host. These would all be among the few wealthier or more socially significant Christians in Corinth. A number of possibilities for abuse could arise from this. These honored guests would also probably be in a position to arrive early and begin eating earlier than the many slaves, laborers, and small business people who would only be able to assemble after the end of their workday. Not only would they not be enjoying the same fine meal as the early arrivals, but among these late arrivals there could be a great disparity in fare, as "each one goes ahead with his own supper, and one goes hungry while another gets drunk" (11:21).

It is only after describing the contempt they show one another in their agape meal that Paul reminds them of the core tradition of the Eucharist that he had handed on to them. We have already seen how closely the words in Paul's eucharistic liturgy resemble those in Luke. The context in this section of First Corinthians tells us that Paul is recalling the true meaning of the Eucharist to shame them for their lack of consideration of each other. When Jesus said, "This is my body that is for you. Do this in remembrance of me" and "This cup is the new covenant in my blood. Do this, as often as you drink it, in remembrance of me," he was revealing that his death on the cross was an act of love intended to unite them with himself in a new covenant with God. This sacrifice of Jesus' self as the ultimate gift of life to his followers, which they are in turn to do in remembrance of him, is utterly incompatible with the Corinthians' selfish behavior during the agape in which they attempt to celebrate Eucharist.

In this context, it is clear that Paul takes the reality that the baptized are the body of Christ (1 Cor 12:13) as truly as he believes the bread and wine of the Eucharist become the Lord's body and blood. The Corinthians' failure to discern "the body" lies chiefly in their failure to recognize each other as the body of Christ. They are intentionally gathering to celebrate Eucharist, but in doing so, ignore the body of Christ assembled for the agape. Paul says, "That is why many among you are ill and infirm, and a considerable number are dying." In a time when healings were prevalent in Christian ministry (1 Cor 12:9), and the expectation that the return of the Lord was imminent, illness and death among these early Christians would have been problematic, as we know from First Thessalonians (4:13-18).

Paul Breaks Bread in Acts

Finally, we turn once again to Luke, as he narrates two final instances of breaking bread in the book of Acts. As we saw earlier, Luke uses the theme to indicate an actual Eucharist, but also to deliberately imbue a meal with eucharistic themes without actually describing a eucharistic celebration. In the passage that immediately follows, set in Troas, to the far northwest of Ephesus on what is now the west coast of Turkey, it is evident that when Paul breaks the bread "on the first day of the week," it tells us that Paul is celebrating the Eucharist. The larger context that frames this narrative is that Paul is returning to Jerusalem after a successful missionary trip to Europe (Paul's third missionary journey), but suspects that it might be dangerous to return there (Acts 19:21; 20:22). What precedes the breaking of the bread, however, is another essential element to Sunday liturgies of all time, a homily. But Paul, in consideration of the fact that he might never see the Troas disciples again, goes on and on with his homily, with nearly tragic results.

Acts 20:7-12

> [7]On the first day of the week when we gathered to break bread, Paul spoke to them because he was going to leave on the next day, and he kept on speaking until midnight. [8]There were many lamps in the upstairs room where we were gathered, [9]and a young man named Eutychus who was sitting on the window sill was sinking into a deep sleep as Paul talked on and on. Once overcome by sleep, he fell down from the third story and when he was picked up, he was dead. [10]Paul went down, threw himself upon him, and said as he embraced him, "Don't be alarmed; there is life in him." [11]Then he returned upstairs,

broke the bread, and ate; after a long conversation that lasted until daybreak, he departed. [12]And they took the boy away alive and were immeasurably comforted.

The next and last time we read of Paul breaking bread in Acts occurs after his return to Jerusalem and his subsequent arrest following a disturbance over false accusations that Paul had brought Gentiles into the temple and defiled it (21:27-28). After appealing his case to Caesar, he is sent under military guard to Rome, but during a voyage by ship across the Adriatic Sea, they encounter hazardous conditions and are eventually shipwrecked. Just prior to that, Paul receives a vision that he will eventually arrive safely in Rome and that no one on board the ship will perish, and after reassuring his captors and encouraging them not to abandon ship, he urges them to eat.

Acts 27:27-36

[27]On the fourteenth night, as we were still being driven about on the Adriatic Sea, toward midnight the sailors began to suspect that they were nearing land. [28]They took soundings and found twenty fathoms; a little farther on, they again took soundings and found fifteen fathoms. [29]Fearing that we would run aground on a rocky coast, they dropped four anchors from the stern and prayed for day to come. [30]The sailors then tried to abandon ship; they lowered the dinghy to the sea on the pretext of going to lay out anchors from the bow. [31]But Paul said to the centurion and the soldiers, "Unless these men stay with the ship, you cannot be saved." [32]So the soldiers cut the ropes of the dinghy and set it adrift.

[33]Until the day began to dawn, Paul kept urging all to take some food. He said, "Today is the fourteenth day that you have been waiting, going hungry and eating nothing. [34]I urge you, therefore, to take some food; it will help you survive. Not a hair of the head of anyone of you will be lost." [35]When he said this, he took bread, gave thanks to God in front of them all, broke it, and began to eat. [36]They were all encouraged, and took some food themselves.

Paul, of course, is not offering the Eucharist to his captors. But Luke is deliberately alluding to the Eucharist by employing the all-important terminology found on the lips of Christ at the feeding of the multitude (Luke 9:16) and at the Last Supper (Luke 22:19) and with the two disciples at Emmaus (Luke 24:30). Paul "took bread, gave thanks to God . . . broke it, and began to eat." A careful reading reveals that Paul feeds himself bread; then, his captors and the ship's crew take encouragement from Paul and feed themselves. By reminding us of the Eucharist, Luke demonstrates that the breaking of bread is an extremely important act of human fellowship, one that resonates with the theme of deliverance. In Paul's apostolic hands and with his prayer and goodwill, the breaking of bread becomes an example that brings safety and renewed life to all, not just to believers.

CHAPTER FIVE

The Eucharist and John's Gospel

John's Version of the Last Supper

Paul and the Synoptic Gospels leave no doubt that the Last Supper was absolutely foundational for what would henceforth be celebrated as the Eucharist. While John's gospel provides the lengthiest theological elaboration on the importance of the Eucharist, there is no direct association between the Eucharist and the Last Supper in John. John 13–14 provides a rich account of the Last Supper, providing details found in no other gospel, most notably that of Jesus washing the disciples' feet before the meal. There is, however, no mention that during the Last Supper Jesus identified himself with bread that was broken for his disciples.

Previously, we took note of the fact that John describes the Last Supper as occurring before the Passover, unlike the Synoptic Gospels, which all indicate that the Last Supper was a Passover meal. Another difference (in some respects, there are more differences between John and the Synoptic Gospels than there are similarities) is that it is only in John that we learn Jesus' ministry spanned three years. We learn this because John mentions three different Passovers during Jesus' ministry (2:13; 6:4; and 12:1). John 6 repeatedly and boldly declares that Jesus offered bread transformed into his own body. John situates this near a Passover a year before Jesus ate his last meal with his disciples. It is only after Jesus and the disciples leave the room where they have eaten the Last Supper that Jesus begins to identify himself with the fruit of the vine, saying that he is the vine that provides life to his followers (15:1-17).

This does not mean that John traces the origin of the Eucharist to a time before the Last Supper. Nor should this lead us to suspect that the

Fourth Gospel was written in ignorance or denial of what would have been, by then, a well-established tradition that the Last Supper was the event from which the Christian Eucharist sprang. As we go through John 6 (below) it should become evident that John's concern for revealing the Eucharist as a gift that fills us with life—eternal life in Christ—was better expressed in a discourse following the feeding of the multitude than during the Last Supper. This is true in part because John's eucharistic theology does not focus on Jesus' passion so much as on Jesus' resurrection. In John, Jesus' death is the moment of his triumph, the moment where he is "raised up," that is, exalted and revealed as king (12:32-33). In John, the power of the resurrection is already evident in Jesus' crucifixion, and so the body of Christ that is given to us in the eucharistic bread brings eternal life to us.

Another plausible reason for John not to include the institution of the Eucharist during the Last Supper is that by the time the Gospel of John was compiled, toward the end of the first century, the celebration of Eucharist was already a matter many Christian communities sought to keep a deeply sacred, private matter. What happened during Eucharist had become increasingly subject to wild rumor among those outside the faith. In some circles Christians were even accused of cannibalism, which seems to be why some of the crowd in John 6 reject Jesus' teaching about the bread of life. The Gospel of John seems to have been written with an awareness of these accusations, and, while boldly affirming the Christian understanding of the Eucharist, preferred not to have the actual words of institution put into the gospel. The words of institution and their connection to the Last Supper would be nothing for which John's community would need instruction.

John, Chapter 6

The revised New Testament of the New American Bible divides John 6 into four sections. The first fifteen verses provide us with John's version of the multiplication of the loaves, which, as in Luke, only occurs once, with the feeding of five thousand "men." John 6:16-21 is John's account of Jesus walking on the water as the disciples are tossed about in a boat. It is interesting that John, whose account of Jesus' ministry is so startlingly different from the other canonical gospels, places the feeding of the five thousand and Jesus walking on the water as tightly together as Matthew (14:13-21, 22-33) and Mark (6:34-44, 45-52). While the majority of scholars believe Matthew had access to Mark's gospel, few suggest that John used either Matthew or Mark.

In John 6:22-59, Jesus is confronted by the crowds he fed in 6:1-15, crowds who would like to enjoy a miraculous gift of bread "always" (6:34). Jesus' response to them is what is known as the "bread of life discourse." This discourse is so explicit about Jesus providing his own body as food that, in the final section (6:60-71), not only do many in the crowd reject Jesus, but many of his own disciples do as well.

It is helpful to keep in mind while reading John 6 that one major part of John's gospel, running from 1:19 through 12:50, is referred to by many scholars as "the book of signs." The first sign, the changing of water to wine at the wedding in Cana, we examined in chapter 2. Scholars usually identify seven signs in the book of signs, each of which is a miraculous deed performed by Jesus. Their function as signs is to lead those with spiritual discernment to a deeper awareness of Jesus' true identity and ultimately to embrace Jesus in faith. The feeding of the five thousand is the fourth sign in the book of signs, and much of Jesus' problem with the crowds during the bread of life discourse is over their failure to look past the sign and encounter in faith the one who gave them the bread.

The Multiplication of the Loaves

John 6:1-15

[1]After this, Jesus went across the Sea of Galilee [of Tiberias]. [2]A large crowd followed him, because they saw the signs he was performing on the sick. [3]Jesus went up on the mountain, and there he sat down with his disciples. [4]The Jewish feast of Passover was near. [5]When Jesus raised his eyes and saw that a large crowd was coming to him, he said to Philip, "Where can we buy enough food for them to eat?" [6]He said this to test him, because he himself knew what he was going to do. [7]Philip answered him, "Two hundred days' wages worth of food would not be enough for each of them to have a little [bit]." [8]One of his disciples, Andrew, the brother of Simon Peter, said to him, [9]"There is a boy here who has five barley loaves and two fish; but what good are these for so many?" [10]Jesus said, "Have the people recline." Now there was a great deal of grass in that place. So the men reclined, about five thousand in number. [11]Then Jesus took the loaves, gave thanks, and distributed them to those who were reclining, and also as much of the fish as they wanted. [12]When they had had their fill, he said to his disciples, "Gather the fragments left over, so that nothing will be wasted." [13]So they collected them, and filled twelve wicker baskets with fragments from the five barley loaves that had been more than they could eat. [14]When the people saw the sign he had done, they said, "This is truly the Prophet, the one who is to come

into the world." ¹⁵Since Jesus knew that they were going to come and carry him off to make him king, he withdrew again to the mountain alone.

The feeding of the five thousand is one of the few miracles for which an account is given in all four canonical gospels. John is unique, however, in telling us that it occurred when "[t]he Jewish feast of Passover was near" (6:4). It is an important detail, far more important than simply an indication of when the feeding took place. The Passover is near and the importance of the Passover to the identity of the Jewish people provides the context for John's account of both the miraculous feeding and Jesus' dialogue with the crowds concerning "the bread of life." Bread is a very important part of Passover. Unleavened bread is not only an essential part of the Passover meal, but, as mentioned in chapter 1, Passover itself had become linked with a seven-day feast of unleavened bread (Exod 23:15). What Passover calls most vividly to mind is the exodus event itself, and so, in telling us that Passover was approaching, John is alerting us to several themes that will grow in importance once the crowds have followed Jesus to Capernaum (6:24).

Though there are crowds following him, before they actually arrive, John tells us that "Jesus went up on the mountain, and there he sat down with his disciples" (6:3). We are then notified that "[t]he Jewish feast of Passover was near" (6:4). In addition to telling us that Passover nears, only John tells us that the feeding took place on a mountain. These two details may be related, in that mountains are prominent places in Scripture for encounters with God, and within Judaism, no encounter on a mountain was as important as that between Moses and God on Sinai, from whence the Ten Commandments were delivered to Israel.

We ought once again to take note of the grass. Indeed, in John, "there was a great deal of grass in that place" (6:10b). As in the Synoptic Gospels, this allusion to Psalm 23 is also important in John: "The Lord is my shepherd; / there is nothing I lack. / In green pastures he makes me lie down" (vv. 1-2a).

Just as the multiplication of the loaves had eucharistic overtones in the Synoptic Gospels, they are no less present in John's gospel. While these themes may not be as prominent here as they will be in the bread of life discourse, the feeding of the multitude provides the necessary foundation for the later discourse.

Scholars note that an important eucharistic allusion unique to John's account can be found in verse 11, where it is Jesus who distributes the loaves and fishes, not the disciples. We noted earlier that in Mark the distribution by the apostles has its own eucharistic connotations, in that after the resurrection it is they who will distribute the Eucharist. But John's narrative has Jesus, the one who first distributed the bread of life, be the one who distributes the bread to the masses.

Scholars also tell us that there is a strong resemblance to the Eucharist as found in the *Didache* in what follows the feeding. Jesus tells his disciples to "[g]ather the fragments" that remained from the meal. In the *Didache* the eucharistic liturgy speaks of fragments of bread (or broken bread) having once been seeds of grain scattered over the mountains and then gathered together to be one. It then asks God to do the same for the church, that is, to gather its members from the ends of the earth and to make them one. Some see John's depiction of Jesus directing the twelve disciples to gather up the fragments in twelve baskets as a sign that they would be the ones to gather in and preserve the church. In 6:12 Jesus commands the gathering of the fragments "so that nothing will be wasted." The word "wasted" can also be translated as "lost." In 6:39 Jesus says of those who will come to him in good faith, "And this is the will of the one who sent me, that I should not lose anything of what he gave me, but that I should raise it [on] the last day."

What that does not tell us is if there is any direct relationship between the eucharistic liturgy found in the *Didache* and how the Eucharist was celebrated in the Johannine community(ies). Eucharistic liturgies in early church communities could have shared a number of elements without sharing similar theological understandings of the Eucharist. There is a great deal of similarity between the accounts of the feeding of the multitude in John, Matthew, Mark, and Luke, yet a majority of scholars believe John's account was derived independently of the Synoptic Gospels. The Gospel of John is absolutely silent about how the Eucharist was celebrated, but there is a very sharp contrast between the eucharistic theology found in John, which complements the gospel's high Christology (meaning it places an emphasis on Jesus' divinity), and the rather low Christology of the *Didache* (it places little emphasis on Jesus' divinity). The eucharistic liturgy in the *Didache* primarily focuses on the Eucharist as that which makes those who celebrate it one with each other in the body of Christ. Little emphasis, if any, is placed on the Eucharist as being the real presence of Christ in his body and blood. As we will see, that is a far cry from the eucharistic theology found within the bread of life discourse (John 6:22-59).

Walking on the Water

John 6:16-21

> [16]When it was evening, his disciples went down to the sea, [17]embarked in a boat, and went across the sea to Capernaum. It had already grown dark, and Jesus had not yet come to them. [18]The sea was stirred up because a strong wind was blowing. [19]When they had rowed about three or four miles, they saw Jesus walking on the sea and coming near the boat, and they began to be afraid. [20]But he said to them, "It is I. Do not be afraid." [21]They wanted to take him into the boat, but the boat immediately arrived at the shore to which they were heading.

As Raymond Brown notes, it is not out of the question that in John's account, Jesus' walking on the waters of the sea is meant to recall the exodus passage from Egypt through sea waters. It might seem like a stretch, but at the same time, the prominence of exodus themes in John 6 makes it difficult to ignore the possibility. The sea is stirred up because of "a strong wind," which may parallel the wind that sweeps over the waters of the sea during the exodus (Exod 14:21-22). In similar accounts in Matthew (14:32) and Mark (4:39), Jesus calms the storm, and his power to do so causes the disciples to either profess faith in him as the Son of God (Matt 14:33) or to ponder the fullness of his identity (Mark 4:41). Here in John, the wind has stirred up the sea, but we don't learn that Jesus calms the storm. Jesus does calm the disciples' fears, however, by revealing himself as divine. "It is I" is *ego eimi* in Greek, which can mean simply "I am," but which can be understood as the name of God (I Am Who I Am; Exod 3:14). This is why the revised New American Bible capitalizes both words later in John when Jesus says "I AM" to those who come with Judas Iscariot to arrest him. We know that Jesus was using the divine name in reference to himself because when he says "I AM," those who have come to arrest him collapse at the power of the name (John 18:5-6). Because of who Jesus is, they are not to be afraid. In the boat the disciples want to "take him in" when they recognize him. The Greek behind the phrase "take him in" is often translated as "receive," as in "they wanted to receive him." This is the all-important response to Jesus, as seen in the New Revised Standard Version's translation of John 1:12: "But to all who received him, who believed in his name, he gave power to become children of God." Who Jesus is and how one is to receive him are at the heart of the matter in the bread of life discourse.

The Bread of Life Discourse

John 6:22-59

²²The next day, the crowd that remained across the sea saw that there had been only one boat there, and that Jesus had not gone along with his disciples in the boat, but only his disciples had left. ²³Other boats came from Tiberias near the place where they had eaten the bread when the Lord gave thanks. ²⁴When the crowd saw that neither Jesus nor his disciples were there, they themselves got into boats and came to Capernaum looking for Jesus. ²⁵And when they found him across the sea they said to him, "Rabbi, when did you get here?" ²⁶Jesus answered them and said, "Amen, amen, I say to you, you are looking for me not because you saw signs but because you ate the loaves and were filled. ²⁷Do not work for food that perishes but for the food that endures for eternal life, which the Son of Man will give you. For on him the Father, God, has set his seal." ²⁸So they said to him, "What can we do to accomplish the works of God?" ²⁹Jesus answered and said to them, "This is the work of God, that you believe in the one he sent." ³⁰So they said to him, "What sign can you do, that we may see and believe in you? What can you do? ³¹Our ancestors ate manna in the desert, as it is written:

'He gave them bread from heaven to eat.'"

³²So Jesus said to them, "Amen, amen, I say to you, it was not Moses who gave the bread from heaven; my Father gives you the true bread from heaven. ³³For the bread of God is that which comes down from heaven and gives life to the world."

³⁴So they said to him, "Sir, give us this bread always." ³⁵Jesus said to them, "I am the bread of life; whoever comes to me will never hunger, and whoever believes in me will never thirst. ³⁶But I told you that although you have seen [me], you do not believe. ³⁷Everything that the Father gives me will come to me, and I will not reject anyone who comes to me, ³⁸because I came down from heaven not to do my own will but the will of the one who sent me. ³⁹And this is the will of the one who sent me, that I should not lose anything of what he gave me, but that I should raise it [on] the last day. ⁴⁰For this is the will of my Father, that everyone who sees the Son and believes in him may have eternal life, and I shall raise him [on] the last day."

⁴¹The Jews murmured about him because he said, "I am the bread that came down from heaven," ⁴²and they said, "Is this not Jesus, the son of Joseph? Do we not know his father and mother? Then how can he say, 'I have come down from heaven'?" ⁴³Jesus answered and said to them, "Stop murmuring among yourselves. ⁴⁴No one can come

to me unless the Father who sent me draw him, and I will raise him on the last day. ⁴⁵It is written in the prophets:

'They shall all be taught by God.'

Everyone who listens to my Father and learns from him comes to me. ⁴⁶Not that anyone has seen the Father except the one who is from God; he has seen the Father. ⁴⁷Amen, amen, I say to you, whoever believes has eternal life. ⁴⁸I am the bread of life. ⁴⁹Your ancestors ate the manna in the desert, but they died; ⁵⁰this is the bread that comes down from heaven so that one may eat it and not die. ⁵¹I am the living bread that came down from heaven; whoever eats this bread will live forever; and the bread that I will give is my flesh for the life of the world."

⁵²The Jews quarreled among themselves, saying, "How can this man give us [his] flesh to eat?" ⁵³Jesus said to them, "Amen, amen, I say to you, unless you eat the flesh of the Son of Man and drink his blood, you do not have life within you. ⁵⁴Whoever eats my flesh and drinks my blood has eternal life, and I will raise him on the last day. ⁵⁵For my flesh is true food, and my blood is true drink. ⁵⁶Whoever eats my flesh and drinks my blood remains in me and I in him. ⁵⁷Just as the living Father sent me and I have life because of the Father, so also the one who feeds on me will have life because of me. ⁵⁸This is the bread that came down from heaven. Unlike your ancestors who ate and still died, whoever eats this bread will live forever." ⁵⁹These things he said while teaching in the synagogue in Capernaum.

The crowds are evidently wondering where Jesus has gone, since they saw his disciples leave without him in the only available boat. When other boats arrive, they board them and set off to find Jesus. It would take a lot of boats to ferry five thousand souls, but John wants us to understand that it is still a crowd that is following Jesus. In telling us of the boats that have arrived, we are reminded of what has just occurred the day before. The "boats came from Tiberias near the place where they had eaten the bread when the Lord gave thanks" (6:23). The root of the word behind "gave thanks" is *eucharisteo* in Greek. John is setting up for us the cause of the tension that will arise between the crowd and Jesus. The crowd has eaten bread, but it is bread for which Jesus gave thanks. When they find Jesus, the crowd will want more bread, but the one who gave thanks is more important than the bread they recently received.

The crowd finds Jesus and wants to know when (and presumably how) he got there. They address him as "Rabbi" (v. 25). This title is another hint that much of what lies behind the give-and-take between the crowd and Jesus is the question of Jesus' identity. When Jesus fed them, they called him "the Prophet, the one who is to come into the world" (v. 14). Neither title is enough to name who Jesus is. As Jesus came by foot on the stormy sea to his disciples, he revealed himself to them. Jesus will attempt to tell the crowd who he is as well, but unlike the disciples in the boat, they do not want to receive him for who he is, although they would welcome more bread. Jesus gave thanks for the bread and fed them with it as a sign of who he is, so that discovering who was in their midst they would no longer spend their lives in the pursuit of "food that perishes but for the food that endures for eternal life, which the Son of Man will give you" (v. 27).

The heart of Jesus' challenge to the crowd is to have them question the meaning of their lives. What is it they are laboring after? It is a formidable challenge. The crowd is filled with ordinary people of the time and region. These are people who have to work an entire day (not just eight hours) just to earn enough to buy the food they need to make it through the next day's labor. Anything more will have to be set aside to tide them through the Sabbath rest, if they are going to honor it. The day before, Jesus fed them in a miraculous fashion, and now that they believe it might be possible to be freed from labor and still eat, they have abandoned their tasks for another day in order to have more of the bread Jesus gave them. But Jesus hasn't come to simply make it easier to live. He has come to offer them a much greater reason to live than the pursuit of perishable bread. The meaning of life is found in food that provides eternal life.

The crowd (is it a single voice speaking for the crowd or does the crowd volley out the same question?) asks what kind of work God is asking them to do in order to obtain this very special bread. Jesus' answer is straightforward: "[B]elieve in the one he sent" (vv. 28-29). To this the crowd asks for another sign, apparently one that will mean being fed once again: "Our ancestors ate manna in the desert, as it is written: / 'He gave them bread from heaven to eat'" (v. 31).

John first turned our attention to exodus themes by telling us in verse 4 that the feast of Passover was approaching. Now the crowd seems to be enticing Jesus to show he is the prophet that the prophet Moses promised would come after him (see Deut 18:15) by giving them manna, the bread from heaven the children of Israel ate during their wandering in the wilderness (Exod 16:32-33). In Numbers we learn that manna was not the most delicious of foods. The people quickly became tired of it and began to demand meat: "The riffraff among them were so greedy for meat that even the Israelites lamented again, 'If only we had meat for food! We remember the fish we used to eat without cost in Egypt, and the cucumbers, the melons, the leeks, the onions, and the garlic. But now we are famished; we have nothing to look forward to but this manna'" (Num 11:4-6).

By Jesus' time manna was thought of quite differently. As found in the book of Wisdom (written not long before the birth of Christ), God's gift of manna had gained the reputation of being a delightful, angelic food imbued with what might be called magical properties: "[Y]ou nourished your people with food of angels / and furnished them bread from heaven, ready to hand, untoiled-for, / endowed with all delights and conforming to every taste. / For this substance of yours revealed your sweetness toward your children, / and serving the desire of the one who received it, / was changed to whatever flavor each one wished" (Wis 16:20-21).

With a double "amen" Jesus assures them that Moses was never able to provide the true bread from heaven, "[f]or the bread of God is that which comes down from heaven and gives life to the world" (John 6:32-33). So far, the crowd is making their own sense out of what Jesus is saying. It sounds to them like he has very special bread to offer them and they will gladly accept it. "Sir, give us this bread always" (v. 34).

When Jesus assures them that he is "the bread of life; whoever comes to me will never hunger, and whoever believes in me will never thirst," Jesus knows that the crowd isn't buying it, but that does not stop him from telling them something even more incredible: "I came down from heaven" (vv. 35, 38). Knowing their incredulity, Jesus tells them in not so many words that the reason they will not come to him to be fed the bread of eternal life is because their hearts aren't open to hear what God is telling them. If they would listen to God, God would send them to Jesus and Jesus would never lose them; he would even raise them up on the last day (vv. 34-40). While verses 35-40 might sound like the Father has preemptively prevented the crowd from believing in Jesus, the end of verse 45 makes it clear that the Father hasn't led them to Jesus because they do not listen to the Father: "Everyone who listens to my Father and learns from him comes to me."

It is a noted feature of John's gospel that Jesus' message is often misinterpreted by those who hear his teachings. In John 3:1-12 we are given a perfect example of how people interpret Jesus' words in an "earthly" manner, and thus fail to gain the necessary spiritual understanding. Jesus tells Nicodemus that "no one can see the kingdom of God without being born from above" (3:3). The Greek "from above" can also mean "again," and so it is when Jesus tells Nicodemus that it is necessary to be born from above, Nicodemus hears something absurd, and asks Jesus, "How can a person once grown old be born again? Surely he cannot reenter his mother's womb and be born again, can he?" (3:4).

Something similar is happening in the dialog between Jesus and the crowd in John 6. The crowd is intent upon hearing about literal bread, the stuff of daily sustenance, even when Jesus tells them that they should seek the true bread from heaven. But then Jesus takes it up a notch and tells them that he is the Bread of Life that has come down from heaven. There are those in the crowd who know Jesus and his family and they consider his talk about having come down from heaven to be ridiculous: "Do we not know his father and mother? Then how can he say, 'I have come down from heaven'?" (6:42). Knowing where Jesus came from is an insight of faith not gained from observing physical reality.

Jesus responds to their objection by returning to a theme from the exodus. "Stop murmuring among yourselves," he tells them in verse 43. When the children of Israel murmured against Moses in the wilderness, God informed them that their entire generation would pass away without entering the Promised Land (Deut 1:27-35). In murmuring against Jesus they risk rejecting the eternal life he, as the Bread of Life, offers them (vv. 48-51).

At this, the crowd begins quarrelling among themselves. "How can this man give us [his] flesh to eat?" (v. 52). The crowd's response tells us that they are taking Jesus too literally. They seem to be picturing in their minds that Jesus is saying he will hack off some of his flesh and serve it to them as a gory, cannibalistic dish. And yet Jesus presses the matter, using the most vivid language possible, almost forcing the crowd to take the most extreme misunderstanding possible: "Amen, amen, I say to you, unless you eat the flesh of the Son of Man and drink his blood, you do not have life within you. Whoever eats my flesh and drinks my blood has eternal life, and I will raise him on the last day" (vv. 53-54). The Greek verb used in verse 54 for "eats" is not the verb used for "eat" in verse 53. The verb for "eat" in verse 54 was, at the time of John's gospel, a cruder word associated with the uncivilized chomping or gnawing of animals greedily gobbling away at their food.

Of course Jesus would be addressing the crowd in Aramaic, not Greek, and so this should tell us that in switching to this more vulgar verb, John is making a theological point. We know from both the first and second letters of John, which are closely associated with the style and theology of John's gospel, that the community(ies) for whom all three were written had to deal with teachings that denied that Jesus was truly human, denying that he, like us, was a flesh-and-blood human being.

"This is how you can know the Spirit of God: every spirit that acknowledges Jesus Christ come in the flesh belongs to God, and every spirit that does not acknowledge Jesus does not belong to God. This is the spirit of the antichrist that, as you heard, is to come, but in fact is already in the world" (1 John 4:2-3).

"Many deceivers have gone out into the world, those who do not acknowledge Jesus Christ as coming in the flesh; such is the deceitful one and the antichrist" (2 John 7).

So, on one level, it can be said that John emphasizes Jesus' flesh-and-blood reality to make certain that Christians who read (or hear) his gospel will be protected against a heresy that arose years after Jesus rose from the dead. But that important understanding takes nothing away from the implications John 6:53-58 have for our understanding of the Eucharist.

Jesus' extremely vivid assertions about the necessity of eating his body and drinking his blood cannot be dissociated from the Eucharist. The words insist upon our eating his body and drinking his blood if we are to have life within us. No Christian of the late first century who heard this could possibly have doubted that Jesus was referring to the Eucharist. Jesus' response to their consternation at being told the bread Jesus offers is his flesh is so graphic that it makes no room for a metaphorical understanding. We see two things being emphasized at once in this section—the glaringly explicit depiction of the fully human reality of the Word of God and an equally bold assertion that in the Eucharist Jesus' followers consume the body and blood of the Lord. Neither assertion can be disentangled from the other.

That is not to say that there were no Christians appalled at the idea that the Eucharist truly presented Jesus' body and blood for our consumption. Those who were wont to believe that Jesus only appeared to come in human form would not have any use for a theology that emphasized Jesus' physical presence in the Eucharist. They would probably react to such a teaching in the same manner as the disciples in verses 60-66. Indeed, the gospel probably intended to account for a split in the Johannine community over this very matter.

The Words of Eternal Life

John 6:60-71

⁶⁰Then many of his disciples who were listening said, "This saying is hard; who can accept it?" ⁶¹Since Jesus knew that his disciples were murmuring about this, he said to them, "Does this shock you? ⁶²What if you were to see the Son of Man ascending to where he was before?

⁶³It is the spirit that gives life, while the flesh is of no avail. The words I have spoken to you are spirit and life. ⁶⁴But there are some of you who do not believe." Jesus knew from the beginning the ones who would not believe and the one who would betray him. ⁶⁵And he said, "For this reason I have told you that no one can come to me unless it is granted him by my Father."

⁶⁶As a result of this, many [of] his disciples returned to their former way of life and no longer accompanied him. ⁶⁷Jesus then said to the Twelve, "Do you also want to leave?" ⁶⁸Simon Peter answered him, "Master, to whom shall we go? You have the words of eternal life. ⁶⁹We have come to believe and are convinced that you are the Holy One of God." ⁷⁰Jesus answered them, "Did I not choose you twelve? Yet is not one of you a devil?" ⁷¹He was referring to Judas, son of Simon the Iscariot; it was he who would betray him, one of the Twelve.

It is hard not to notice how stunningly different Jesus speaks in John when compared with the Synoptic Gospels. He doesn't teach in parables in John, and many of the signs (or miracles) in John either aren't found in the Synoptics or are presented in a far different manner. Jesus' ministry begins with the sign of the water turned to wine at the wedding in Cana and he raises Lazarus from the dead just before being arrested. These signs are like bookends surrounding Jesus' ministry, and yet they are not even mentioned in the other gospels.

And yet, for all the differences, there are some stunning parallels, all the more stunning because of the differences. In Matthew 15:32-39 we read the second account of Jesus feeding a multitude from just a few loaves of bread. Matthew's account bears a strong likeness to Mark's account in 8:1-10. In both Matthew and Mark, this feeding of a multitude is followed by a demand for a sign from Jesus by some Pharisees and Sadducees (Matt 16:1-4; Mark 8:11-13). Jesus and his disciples then travel by boat on the Sea of Galilee (Matt 16:5-12; Mark 8:14-21). Shortly afterward, Peter makes his confession of faith (Matt 16:13-20; Mark 8:27-30).

While the differences are undeniable, it also seems very unlikely that John's account of Jesus feeding the multitude, crossing the Sea of Galilee, and being confronted by a demand for a sign that is followed up by a confession of faith by Peter comes from a tradition unrelated to that found in Matthew and Mark. But the similarities beneath the accounts only accentuate the differences that reveal John's highly developed theology. After many disciples leave Jesus because of his insistence that they must eat and drink of his body and blood, he asks Peter and the remaining disciples if they, too, are going to leave him. Peter then confesses loyalty to Jesus by saying, "Master, to whom shall we go? You have the words of eternal life. We have come to believe and are convinced that you are the Holy One of God" (6:68-69). Peter's faith in Jesus springs from his recognition that only Jesus' words offer eternal life. Jesus has just created dissension among the disciples by linking eternal life to eating and drinking his body and blood. In John, Peter's confession of faith in Jesus as the Holy One of God is a eucharistic faith.

Breakfast with the Risen Lord

John 21:1-14

> ¹After this, Jesus revealed himself again to his disciples at the Sea of Tiberias. He revealed himself in this way. ²Together were Simon Peter, Thomas called Didymus, Nathanael from Cana in Galilee, Zebedee's sons, and two others of his disciples. ³Simon Peter said to them, "I am going fishing." They said to him, "We also will come with you." So they went out and got into the boat, but that night they caught nothing. ⁴When it was already dawn, Jesus was standing on the shore; but the disciples did not realize that it was Jesus. ⁵Jesus said to them, "Children, have you caught anything to eat?" They answered him, "No." ⁶So he said to them, "Cast the net over the right side of the boat and you will find something." So they cast it, and were not able to pull it in because of the number of fish. ⁷So the disciple whom Jesus loved said to Peter, "It is the Lord." When Simon Peter heard that it was the Lord, he tucked in his garment, for he was lightly clad, and jumped into the sea. ⁸The other disciples came in the boat, for they were not far from shore, only about a hundred yards, dragging the net with the fish. ⁹When they climbed out on shore, they saw a charcoal fire with fish on it and bread. ¹⁰Jesus said to them, "Bring some of the fish you just caught." ¹¹So Simon Peter went over and dragged the net ashore full of one hundred fifty-three large fish. Even though there were so many, the net was not torn. ¹²Jesus said to them, "Come, have breakfast." And none of the disciples dared to ask him, "Who are you?" because they realized it was the Lord. ¹³Jesus came over and took the bread and gave it to them, and in like manner the fish. ¹⁴This was now the third time Jesus was revealed to his disciples after being raised from the dead.

Immediately following this scene, we read again that what the disciples were eating with the risen Lord was, quite simply, "breakfast" (21:15). But what a breakfast: a meal of bread and fish prepared and served for them by the risen Lord himself! This is not the only account of the risen

Christ eating fish with his disciples. There is also this one in Luke: " 'Why are you troubled? And why do questions arise in your hearts? Look at my hands and my feet, that it is I myself. Touch me and see, because a ghost does not have flesh and bones as you can see I have.' And as he said this, he showed them his hands and his feet. While they were still incredulous for joy and were amazed, he asked them, 'Have you anything here to eat?' They gave him a piece of baked fish; he took it and ate it in front of them" (24:38-43).

There is no telling if these two quite different accounts spring from a single original tradition. It seems more likely that there was more than one tradition of Jesus eating with his disciples after the resurrection. In Acts, for example, Peter proclaims the good news of Jesus' resurrection to the eager Gentile Cornelius and indicates that eating with the risen Christ was not all that uncommon for the apostles: "We are witnesses of all that he did both in the country of the Jews and [in] Jerusalem. They put him to death by hanging him on a tree. This man God raised [on] the third day and granted that he be visible, not to all the people, but to us, the witnesses chosen by God in advance, who ate and drank with him after he rose from the dead" (10:39-41).

For a century or more there have been scholars who have debated whether the risen Christ would have had a body of such a nature that it would actually digest food. Such speculation is beyond the competence of any theologian this side of the grave. It also entirely misses an essential truth about the risen Christ—that he is with us, he is in our midst, and when we eat together in his name we are having fellowship with him. That was the essence of the early agape meals, which sadly came to be abused. In our day-to-day fellowship with each other we may not actually be seeing Christ in person, but we are shortsighted if we are not seeing him in each other.

Conclusion

In beginning this commentary on the story of the Eucharist in Scripture, I deliberately set out to trace a line from the Old Testament to the New Testament that connected the importance of simply eating to the almost unimaginable reality of receiving the body and blood of Christ in the appearance of bread and wine. The connection is one I hope we will always bear in our minds and hearts. Being creatures, we cannot live without food and drink, and yet knowing that we are *creatures* ought always to remind us that we are the handiwork of the *Creator*, and so is the food we eat. Eating is an act to be undertaken in full consciousness that our very existence is a gift of the Creator and the daily renewal of our lives is a gift of the Creator. Our lack of constant recognition of this is, in part, a reminder that although we are pure gift, we are also in need of redemption, for we have fallen short in offering our love with all our heart, all our soul, and all our strength to God in gratitude (Mark 12:30). It is no coincidence that when God chose to redeem us through the life, death, and resurrection of his Son, he gave us his Son fully present as food, the sacrament that nurtures in us the same eternal life that is the Son's.

It would be a great reward for me if more than a few readers of this commentary discovered that the simple act of eating was never quite so simple again. May we always eat with hearts that give thanks. Ultimately, however, I hope your participation in the Eucharist will be even more closely associated with the Word of God. "[I]t is not by bread alone that people live, but by all that comes forth from the mouth of the LORD" (Deut 8:3). The new Roman Missal provides us with something magnificent to contemplate in our participation in the Eucharist, and provides a fitting conclusion to this commentary on the story of Eucharist in Scripture.

You are indeed Holy and to be glorified, O God,
who love the human race
and who always walk with us on the journey of life.
Blessed indeed is your Son,
present in our midst
when we are gathered by his love,
and when, as once for the disciples, so now for us,
he opens the Scriptures and breaks the bread.
(Eucharistic Prayer for Use in Masses for Various Needs I, II, III, and IV)

Welcome to the feast!

Suggested Readings

Brown, Raymond E. *The Gospel according to John I–XII.* The Anchor Bible. Garden City, NY: Doubleday, 1966.

Brueggemann, Walter. *Isaiah 1–39.* Edited by Patrick D. Miller and David L. Bartlett. Louisville, KY: Westminster John Knox Press, 1998.

Collins, Raymond F. *First Corinthians.* Edited by Daniel J. Harrington. Sacra Pagina Series. Collegeville, MN: Liturgical Press, 1999.

Johnson, Luke Timothy. *The Acts of the Apostles.* Edited by Daniel J. Harrington. Sacra Pagina Series. Collegeville, MN: Liturgical Press, 1992.

Karris, Robert J. *Eating Your Way Through Luke's Gospel.* Collegeville, MN: Liturgical Press, 2006.

Kodell, Jerome. *The Eucharist in the New Testament.* Edited by Mary Ann Getty. Zacchaeus Studies: New Testament Series. Wilmington, DE: Michael Glazier, 1988.

LaVerdiere, Eugene. *The Beginning of the Gospel: Introducing the Gospel According to Mark—Volume 1.* Collegeville, MN: Liturgical Press, 1999.

———. *The Breaking of the Bread: The Development of the Eucharist according to Acts.* Chicago: Liturgical Training Publications, 1998.

———. *Dining in the Kingdom of God: The Origins of the Eucharist according to Luke.* Chicago: Liturgical Training Publications, 1994.

———. *The Eucharist in the New Testament and the Early Church.* Collegeville, MN: Liturgical Press, 1996.

Lohfink, Gerhard. "Did Jesus Die for 'Many' or for 'All'?" Chapter 7 in *No Irrelevant Jesus: On Jesus and the Church Today.* Translated by Linda M. Maloney. Collegeville, MN: Liturgical Press, 2014.

Malina, Bruce. "Kinship and Marriage, Fusing Families Together." Chapter 5 in *The New Testament World, Revised Edition.* Louisville, KY: Westminster/John Knox Press, 1993.

Moloney, Francis J. *A Body Broken for a Broken People: Eucharist in the New Testament, Revised Edition.* Peabody, MA: Hendrickson Publishers, 1997.

———. *The Gospel of John.* Edited by Daniel J. Harrington. Sacra Pagina Series. Collegeville, MN: Liturgical Press, 1998.

Murphy-O'Connor, Jerome. "House Churches and the Eucharist." Part 3 in *St. Paul's Corinth: Texts and Archaeology, Third Revised and Expanded Edition.* Collegeville, MN: Liturgical Press, 2002.